LOOKING BACK AT

FASHION
1901·1939

21116804N

TS

LOOKING BACK AT

FASHION
1901·1939

Von Whiteman

EP Publishing Limited 1978

Copyright © 1978 Von Whiteman

This edition first published 1970
by EP Publishing Limited
East Ardsley, Wakefield, West Yorkshire,
England

ISBN: 0 7158 1206 8

ep

Please address all enquiries to:
EP Publishing Limited (address as above)

Printed by G. Beard & Son Ltd,
Brighton, Sussex

Contents

A fashion parade in 1925

A Perpetual Summer: 1900-1907

What sort of clothes are you wearing at the moment? If you look at yourself in front of a full-length mirror, you will see that you probably wear a top of some kind (a T-shirt, jersey or shirt) with a skirt or trousers, tights or socks, and shoes. Underneath you could have on any of the following: pants, maybe worn with a vest, if you are a boy; pants, perhaps with a slip, vest or bra if you are a girl. Many of your clothes will be made from man-made or 'synthetic' fibres with names like Courtelle, Acrylic or Polyester, or they might be natural wool or cotton. Imagine yourself putting them on first thing in the morning and taking them off at night. With the help of a zip here and a button there you can slip in and out of them easily. Many of the clothes we wear are called 'easy-care' because they are designed to be worn, washed, dried and worn again with the minimum of washing and ironing. The same applies to your parents' clothes; they are probably not very different from your own, apart from their more formal clothes such as smart daytime suits and dressy outfits for the evening.

When you find out how your great-grandparents dressed you will begin to realise how things have changed during the last eighty years. The figures staring out at you from old family photographs look stiff and formal, but very picturesque. It is not just by chance that they look the way they do. Their elaborate clothes reflect how they felt about themselves as men and women, about their attitudes to health and modesty, and about their position in the world. You can see for yourself, from these photographs, that at the beginning of this century people looked and felt very secure, whatever their place in life. And yet, during the twentieth century, the most extraordinary upheavals have transformed their way of living. There have been two World Wars; women have begun to find their freedom and a new place in society; we now think more carefully about the needs of our bodies, and about the importance of fresh air and exercise. Enormous advances in technology—some good, some not so good—have been made. Telephones, radio and television, cars and aeroplanes, labour-saving devices of all kinds have made life move at a speed which anyone back in 1900 would not have believed possible. And many of the tremendous changes which have influenced the way we live nowadays happened in the short space of thirty-nine years between 1900 and the start of the Second World War in 1939.

When Queen Victoria died in 1901, the dreary official atmosphere which had hung over the country for the last part of her reign came to a welcome end. Sixty-four years, after all, is a very long time to reign. And since the death of her beloved husband and consort Prince Albert in 1861 the Queen had chosen to live a quiet, secluded life of deep mourning. She only appeared in public for her people to cheer her at her Jubilee celebrations in 1887 and again at the Diamond Jubilee of 1897. So her subjects might be forgiven for almost

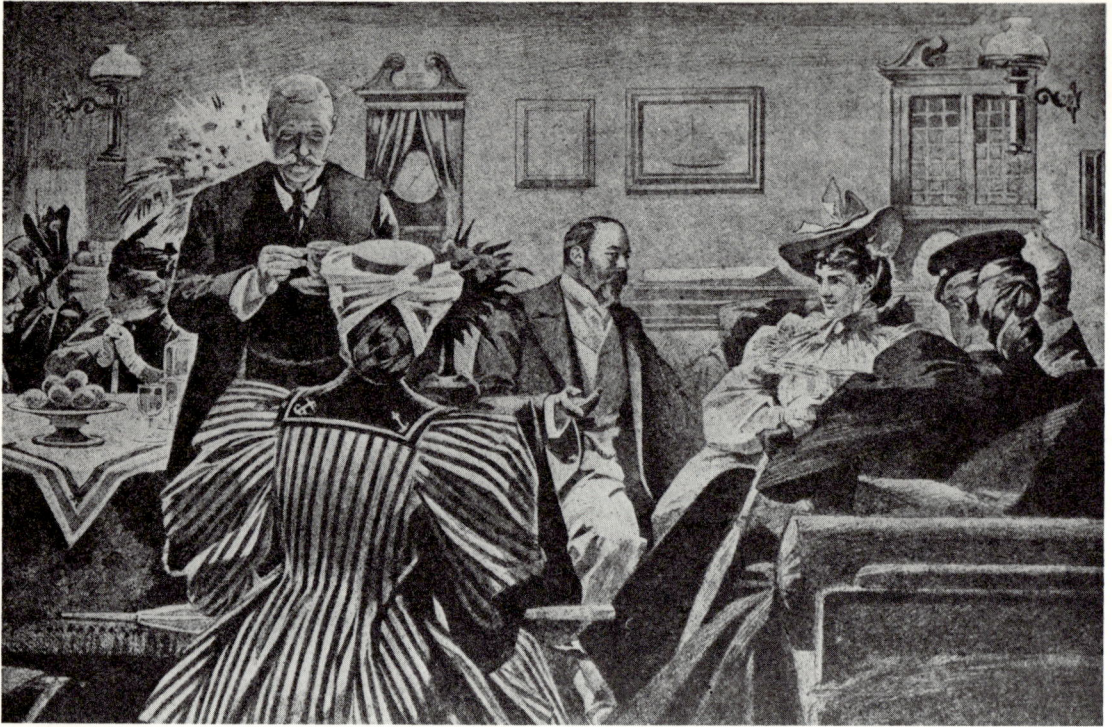

The Prince of Wales taking tea on his yacht the Britannia, *1894*

forgetting that they even had a Queen! Unfortunately for her eldest son, Edward the Prince of Wales, she stubbornly refused to allow him to take over any of her more important State duties during the latter part of her reign, even when he was a grown man and married. So Prince Edward, unable to do anything useful, filled in his endless hours of boredom with a round of gaiety and amusement. He gathered around him a fun-loving circle of aristocratic men and women, known as the Marlborough Set (for at this time the Prince was living at Marlborough House in Pall Mall). When his mother died and he came to the Throne of England with Alexandra as his Queen, King Edward VII's distinguished group of friends moved into the social limelight with him. For the next few years his Court circle led the fashionable Edwardian world in all matters of taste and fashion.

They were years of great splendour, luxury and what has been called 'a perpetual summer' among the upper classes in England and throughout Europe. In those days, no matter what the time of year, there were always fashionable places to go and smart occasions on which to be seen, if you were rich enough to enjoy a life of leisure. One newspaper of the time, advising its readers where they should spend their time, wrote:

> There are the London season, from the middle of May to August; the German-Bath season, from August to the middle of September; the country-house season, from the middle of September to the middle of December; and the South of France season, from the middle of December to the middle of May.[1]

The 'German-Bath' season consisted of taking the waters—that is, drinking and bathing in the health-giving mineral waters of Bath Spa or Marienbad. The Edwardians loved their food. So after over-taxing their livers with an excess of banquets and bouts of drinking, they went to the health spas to recover before returning to England, where they would start stuffing themselves again!

During the country-house visits which

made up the autumn season you were required to change your clothes for each meal and for each new activity. These could amount to as many as half a dozen changes of clothes in a day. One fashionable lady of those days recalled:

We were for ever changing our clothes, a custom which necessitated travelling with a mountain of luggage—at least one large domed trunk called a Noah's Ark, an immense hat box and a heavy fitted dressing case. Winter was the worst season for changing. You came down to breakfast in your "best dress", usually made of velvet, and after Church changed into tweeds. Another "change" for tea—those who possessed that specialised creation—into a "tea-gown"; the less affluent into a summer day-dress. However small your dress allowance, a different dinner gown was considered essential for each evening. Thus a Friday to Monday party involved taking your "Sunday Best", two tweed coats and skirts, three garments suitable for tea, your "best hat"—usually a vast affair loaded with feathers, fruit or corn—a variety of country headgear, as likely as not a billycock hat and riding habit, numerous accessories in the way of petticoats, stoles, scarves, evening wreaths and what not; and a large bag in which to carry about the house your embroidery . . .[2]

Even at the end of their reign, aged 66, Queen Alexandra was a most elegant woman

It was not 'done' for the same outfit to be seen twice during your stay, so you can imagine how many piles of luggage would be unloaded from your carriage for even a few days' visiting. Needless to say, large numbers of servants were needed to run around fetching and carrying, attending and dressing their masters and mistresses. In those days servants were cheap to employ and easy to hire; respectable girls from poor families had no other choice than to 'go into service'. So they went with great parties of fashionable people who were forever moving between town and country, from England to France and Germany, from hunting and shooting expeditions in Scotland to yachting at Cowes, from dinners to grand balls in London—all following the King in his untiring search for amusement. Kind Edward's circle differed from the previous, stuffy Victorian court: although he was obliged to surround himself with the titled aristocracy of England, he also welcomed more exotic personalities from other walks of life. If they were amusing or attractive enough, he chose to overlook their unconventional backgrounds. Many rich and beautiful American heiresses who had married English peers were entertained by the King, a number of successful actresses were drawn into his circle, and even a few men who worked in the middle-class world of trade and finance entered high society. Such things would have been unheard-of in Queen Victoria's reign. Yet, even though the cream of society had changed a little, the formal etiquette it observed remained as strict as ever.

Queen Alexandra was a stunningly beautiful woman, well-suited to lead the fashion world, with a regal manner and natural good taste. She also had a mind of her own. At the ball to celebrate their Coronation in 1901 she amazed everyone by making her entrance in a light-coloured gown, at a time when everyone else was dressed in dark mourning for the late Queen Victoria. From that moment on, whatever she wore set the style for her court to follow: it was she who introduced the soft pastel and sweet pea shades of pink, pale blue,

Corsets et Jupons

Jupon en très bon taffetas uni et glacé, toutes nuances, haut volant nervuré et gansé. **29.50**

Corset en très beau coutil, fond écru broché ciel ou rose, véritable baleine, 4 jarretelles . . **16.50**

Corset en batiste brochée, forme nouvelle, véritable baleine, blanc, ciel ou rose, 4 jarretelles . . . . **27.** »

La Néa brevetée, Nouvelle ceinture sangle du Dr Glénard, en coutil satiné, ciel, rose ou blanc, caoutchouc ajouré.
Hauteur 0^m.16. **24.50**
Hauteur 0^m.20. **27.75**

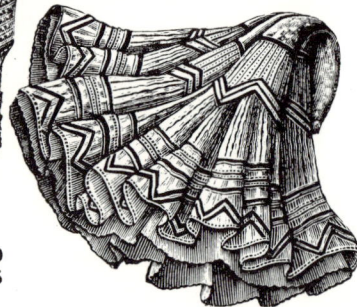

Advertisement for Edwardian underpinnings: S-shaped corsets and taffeta petticoats

lilac and creamy yellow which were so popular throughout the early nineteen-hundreds. Fashionable society went to the Paris *couturiers* (high class designers and dress-makers) such as Worth, Callot and Paquin for their gowns, but Queen Alexandra felt as strongly patriotic about her clothes as she did about everything else, and she was dressed mainly by London couture houses. Even in her sixties she still looked 'dazzlingly beautiful, whether in gold and silver by night, or in violet velvet by day' and she 'succeeded in making every other woman look common beside her'.[3]

In those days there were no film stars or models to set fashion trends. Society ladies tried to copy the elegant dress of women such as the actress Lily Langtry, or the facial expression of the American performer Maxine Elliott (she was called a 'professional beauty' because she allowed her portrait to be used for advertisements and to be sold as a picture postcard). Famous variety artistes attracted crowds to their first night performances as much for the stylish Paris fashions they wore as for their singing and dancing. Lily Elsie, star of the successful operetta 'The Merry Widow', made everybody who saw her want to start waltzing, and she started a fashion for enormous Merry Widow hats. The lovely women who made up a variety act called the Gaiety Girls were seen at all the best places 'wearing gorgeous creations of crêpe de Chine, chiffon, or lace over petticoats of rustling silk edged with hundreds of yards of fine Valenciennes lace threaded with narrow velvet ribbon. Every stitch was sewn by hand and no *couturier* of repute would have dreamed of copying a model gown'.[4]

A well known variety artiste, Marie Studholme, dressed for the stage

Women's clothes

The nineteen-hundreds were the last years when a mature female figure was every woman's ideal. Men described the women they admired as having 'hour-glass' figures, or as being 'Junoesque' (after the matronly curves of the Roman goddess Juno). To emphasise her curves a woman would lace herself tightly into an extraordinary S-shaped corset. This strange foundation garment forced her bosom forward and her hips back, giving the impression that she had an enormous one-piece bosom, which was jokingly referred to as a 'monobosom'. In those days, if you showed even a hint of cleavage you were considered most immodest. Women who wanted to make their bosoms look even larger wore frilly camisole bodices or added boned

shaping; they even used handkerchiefs to pad out their natural shape. They would then pouch out their blouses over tight-waisted bell-shaped skirts which fell to the ground and trailed along behind them. For walking they either wore slightly shorter skirts or used little clips to hitch up the extra length so that their skirt would not collect dust. These skirts had all sorts of exotic names. The 'Waterfall' skirt was gathered in tucks around the hips, then pleated into the waist-band at the back with the fullness falling in a waterfall shape behind. The 'Mermaid' skirt hugged the hips and thighs tightly, then flared out from the knees at the back; when it was pulled round the feet in a swirling spiral it looked like a fish tail. The 'Umbrella' skirt was cut in two semi-circles shaped to the hips and full below the knees. Under their skirts women wore foundation underskirts, often containing a pocket or two, and made of beautiful taffeta or organdie, that rustled when they walked. One of the most popular makes of underskirt was the 'Invincible', which sold for eight shillings and sixpence and could be ordered by mail; you could choose from a variety of gaudy colours and the makers guaranteed that the 'Invincible' would swish loudly when you walked. If the skirt worn over the underskirt was of a lightweight fabric, then it would be weighted around the hem with small lead weights. Like all Edwardian clothes, women's skirts were usually elaborately trimmed with tucks, braid, inserted pleats and box-pleats.

Seeing a group of Edwardian women dressed for a social occasion you would have thought they were a fleet of ships in full sail, carrying all before them. The effect when they moved was very stately, mainly because they wore so many undergarments beneath their clothes, which prevented them from moving fast. Next to her bare skin a woman would wear a chemise, over that a tightly-laced corset in its corset cover, then drawers, a flannel petticoat, several cotton petticoats and finally a splendid silk underskirt as a smooth base for her day or evening gown.

To give you some idea of the extravagance of Edwardian women's dress, imagine for a moment gowns made of frothy chiffon and delicate lace, soft fabrics such as mohair and cashmere, silks with exotic names like tussore, soft faille, net and ninon—all trimmed with frills, beads, pom-poms and frogging. Evening wear was even more sumptuous than day dress. Women often exposed their shoulders in off-the-shoulder gowns, or wore transparent or lacy sleeves trimmed with flounces, ruffles and puffs. The waist seam on their dresses would be in the natural place at the front, but would be drawn up several inches at the back to emphasise the bloused-over, top-heavy effect of the S-bend corset. As for their evening skirts, the hems flared out full over their feet, trailing away at the back in a train lined underneath with a froth of lace or chiffon. When we read about the suggested trimmings of the time, we begin to realise how plain our own clothes are by comparison:

> Garnitures of pearls, groups of tinsel butterflies or dragonflies, and *choux* (rosettes) of velvet or satin, edged with pearly or coral beads, are favourite adornments. White lace robes are encrusted with appliqués of black lace, and black lace robes with the heavier type of Venicepoint in cream or écru.[5]

To balance their thrown-back, S-shaped figures, women built their hair up and out over 'rats'—pads which were inserted under the hair to make it look a bigger shape all round. The hair at the back was then drawn up and pinned with carved ivory, tortoiseshell or horn combs. This was an age when yards of long hair were considered to be a woman's crowning glory, to be brushed a hundred times a day with silver or ivory-backed brushes. However, for those women whose hair was not as thick and long as they might like, a length of false hair (called a 'transformation') could easily be pinned under their own hair. Some women wore a hair-piece in the fashion set by Queen Alexandra and known as a 'Royal Fringe'. On top of their coiffures they suspended enormous cartwheel hats festooned with birds and flowers, which were held in place with long sharp jewelled hat pins. And the fur and feathers they wore! —curls of waving ostrich, osprey and aigrette

plumes, artificial flowers, trailing fur stoles, marabou boas, enormous pillowy muffs for chilly weather. Even in summer, a lady never went out without gloves and a frilly little parasol, which served both as a fashion accessory and to keep the sun from browning her face, for in those days a white skin was thought to be a sign of great beauty and gentility in a woman. Only 'common' people who worked out in the open air had sunburnt faces and rough ungloved hands. It was thought 'fast', almost indecent, to wear cosmetics of any kind, but in fact many fashionable women followed the example of the professional and acting beauties and discreetly applied a little makeup. This might be a leaf of *papier poudré* (ground rice powder) which helped to tone down a shiny nose, or it might be rouge or even dark *kohl* (an eastern powder) to enhance the eyes. Back in the 1890s the writer Max Beerbohm noted, 'most women are not as young as they are painted'.[6]

Women's shoes in those early days were high-cut with a medium heel, strapped and buckled or barred and buttoned. When they were going out walking they would put on sturdy lace-up Oxford or Derby-style shoes. Black leather was worn in winter, white in summer. Evening shoes, like evening clothes, were more elaborate, often made of beaded and decorated brocade or *glacé* (glossy) leather. A rich woman would wear stockings of fine ribbed silk or warm cashmere, but for a more humble woman, cotton lisle stockings had to do.

By the beginning of the twentieth century bridge was a popular tea-time parlour game. Edwardian women wore special clothes for every occasion, and playing bridge was no exception. The 'bridge frock' was an elaborate afternoon dress or skirt; over it you wore a 'bridge coat' of lace, brocade or velvet. Strangely enough, you did not wear a 'tea-gown' for tea, but later on in the evening, if you were dining quietly at home. Tea-gowns were perhaps the most elegant garment of the Edwardian age. They were cut rather more loosely than other forms of dress (unless you include the billowing night-gowns that

Tea gowns, as advertised in an early Harrods catalogue

women wore in those days) and relied for their effect on complicated draping, with trimmings concentrated mainly at the sleeves, wrists and hem. The Italian designer Fortuny was renowned for his exquisite tea-gowns which were instantly recognisable by the minute accordion pleating he loved to sew around the edges. But women liked wearing tea-gowns for reasons other than their dainty appearance: under the loose draping a woman could undo her corset lacings and relax—even breathe— a little! The great French actress Sarah Bernhardt used to wear a tea-gown without a corset underneath, which led to scandalised comments from other women, but delighted her male admirers. She was in many ways a pioneer of women's physical freedom: she even designed and wore her own version of a man's trouser suit!

During the late nineteenth century the Rational Dress Society was founded to try and

Lady Sarah Wilson, a 'New Woman', out climbing, dressed in her tailor-made

15

make women's clothing more comfortable to wear, by doing away with tight lacing, trailing skirts and high heels. Its leaders recommended 'that the maximum weight of underclothing should not exceed seven pounds'. (Nowadays, your underclothes probably weigh less than half a pound!) By trying to change their restrictive ways of dressing, pioneering women hoped to make the public recognise how much they needed to improve their position in society. Eventually they hoped to obtain, by Acts of Parliament, the same rights as men. So they set about founding and improving girls' schools, and campaigning to establish places for women in the universities. Already, in what had always been considered a man's world, a few middle-class, educated women were now following careers: typewriting, compositing, operating telegraph services and working in telephone exchanges and Post Offices. In 1880 the ABC chain of tea shops opened and in 1884 the Ladies' Lavatory Company opened the first decent ladies' lavatory at Oxford Circus, both set up to cater for professional working women. During the nineteen-hundreds for the first time women were able to dine outside their own homes without being regarded as going beyond the pale. The Savoy Hotel, opened in 1889, was the first establishment where women could meet comfortably for dinner and supper. This fashion for dining in restaurants gave women another excuse for wearing elegant evening clothes.

Now that the safety bicycle was on sale everywhere, women were able to make their own way about town instead of having to rely on being driven around. Bicycling became such a popular pastime for women that even the music halls commented on it:

Some folks think bicycling a thing
A girl should not go in for;
But their idea of fun for one
I do not care a pin for!
So if your figure's trim and slim
Put on your knickerbockers
And shut your ears to cheers and jeers
From rude street-Arab mockers.[7]

Are they ladies or gentlemen? An early cartoon showing Rational Dress

The Gibson Girl wearing the tailored blouse and skirt that was to set the fashion for women everywhere

The 'New Woman', as the better educated, bold-spirited woman was called, wore a new form of dress to symbolise her growing freedom. The 'tailor-made' (the French called it an *amazone*) was not designed originally for New Women at all, but for the fashionable women of the Prince of Wales's yachting circle. However, New Women liked its masculine styling and the tweedy, practical cloth it was made from. In its early days the suit looked more like a flowing riding habit than anything else, but gradually the style was modified to give greater freedom when walking or riding a bicycle. At least, the Edwardians thought it gave them more freedom. But to us, the number of clothes considered decent and suitable for bicycling seems never-ending. Here is a list of the garments which a young girl saw her bicycling companion put on to go out one morning:

Thick, long-legged, long-sleeved woollen combinations.
Over them, white cotton combinations, with plenty of buttons and frills.
Very serious, bony, grey stays, with suspenders.
Black woollen stockings.
White cotton drawers, with buttons and frills.
White cotton 'petticoat-bodice', with embroidery, buttons and frills.
Rather short, white flannel petticoat.
Long alpaca petticoat, with flounces round the bottom.
Pink flannel blouse.
High, starched, white collar, fastened on with studs.
Navy-blue tie.
Blue skirt, touching the ground, and fastened tightly to the blouse with a safety-pin behind.
Leather belt, very tight.
High button boots.[8]

17

The tailor-made look became more popular when a well-known American artist, Charles Dana Gibson, created a character who was soon seen adorning posters and papers everywhere. She was known as the 'Gibson Girl' and her uniform was a tailor-made blouse and skirt. Following her example, women wore tailor-mades, (sometimes with divided skirts) to look trim and business-like, but also for sports—badminton, ballooning, cricket, hockey, skating, croquet, golf, tennis, riding, archery, fishing and climbing. Over their tailor-mades they wore coats which were a version of men's 'ulsters' or overcoats.

Bathing was becoming an increasingly respectable form of exercise. Women and men swam, for modesty's sake, on separate beaches, but in 1901 Bexhill-on-Sea daringly advertised 'mixed bathing' on its beaches. Not that women or their daughters needed to worry about appearing immodest when they went swimming; how could they, when they wore a mob cap, a dark-coloured heavy serge knee-length skirt and tunic over long knickers, together with thick stockings and shoes laced cross-cross up to the knee? For that matter, how could a woman hope to make the most of all her new-found activities, even in a 'tailor-made', with tight corsets pressing in on her rib-cage and pelvis? We can only admire the way our great-grandmothers accomplished what they did wearing the clothes of the time.

For a rich woman, it was easy enough to dress in the elaborate manner demanded by high fashion: she merely visited or sent detailed requirements to a *couturier* such as Worth, at his sumptuous showrooms in Paris, or to Doucet or Paquin, or to Redfern or Henry Creed in London. But for middle-class and poorer women who longed to dress in the latest mode but could not afford the top

Daring young women promenading in bloomers on the quay at Boulogne

prices, the answer was to select a dress design from a glossy magazine, then turn to a local dressmaker round the corner who, with her little Singer manual sewing machine, would run up a new gown quite cheaply. Sometimes these dressmakers worked at home; sometimes they were hired by a household to bring up to date last season's clothes and make general alterations. In one Edwardian novel, the heroine has done just this to her 'Other Dress':

> Would you like to know what I've done to it? I've cut the point into a square, and taken four yards out of the skirt; the chiffon off my wedding-dress has been made into kimono sleeves; then I'm going to wear my wedding-veil as a sort of scarf thrown carelessly over the shoulders; and I've turned the pointed waist-band round, so that it's quite *right* and short-waisted at the back now . . .[9]

Women often made their own underwear at home, or had it hand-stitched for their wedding trousseau by nuns. Paper patterns were first introduced in America in the eighteen-fifties and by the nineteen-hundreds were sold through fashion magazines by such companies as Butterick and Weldons. Magazines like *The Lady* and *The Queen* were widely circulated and in them women could find out both how to dress and where to be seen in town to best advantage. Even those women who were too poor to buy new dresses or remake their old outfits could refurbish their out-of-date dresses with the latest and most fashionable trimmings, year after year. In those days the poor were very poor indeed, for there were no social services and only a few charities organised by wealthy ladies to distribute discarded clothes to them. So for the penniless men and women of the 1900s, darned and patched hand-me-downs and rags were the nearest they ever got to high fashion.

Men's clothes

While Edwardian women's dress sometimes went to absurd extremes, men's clothes remained almost as conservative as they had been during Queen Victoria's reign. Etiquette decided right down to the last button what was correct for every occasion. But between 1900 and 1914 men's clothes were slowly influenced by the trend towards more casual wear for sports and leisure activities. And as social conventions gradually relaxed a little, so did notions of what could be worn for each occasion. For official and formal engagements a gentleman would wear a black or grey frock coat (double-breasted, with two or three buttons on each side of the coat front, flaring open below the waist) worn over a light or matching waistcoat, together with matching, striped or dogstooth trousers. The trousers worn in the early nineteen-hundreds were narrow-legged and extended over the boot or shoe at the bottom front. Younger, fashionable men who wanted to cut a dash were replacing the frock coat with a morning coat (single-breasted with three or four buttons on each side and high lapels, the coat front cut to slope away below the waist and the tails ending behind at the bend of the knee). At court, gentlemen wore a magnificent outfit on ceremonial occasions: a black, claret or mulberry gold-trimmed velvet frock or tail coat, black velvet breeches, a black or white waistcoat, white silk stockings, shoes, white gloves, white bow-tie or ruffles, with a cocked hat and sword!

Max Beerbohm was a great dandy of the time. His self-caricatures nearly always show him 'with a high stiff collar, gloves, a carefully tilted silk hat, a cane, a *boutonnière* (buttonhole bloom), and artfully bulging frock coat, tapering trousers'.[10] The frock coat bulged 'artfully' because he had a clever tailor who cut the coat so that it gave to its wearer a neat-waisted, shapely-hipped silhouette. At the turn of the century many men were still observing the Victorian custom of wearing stays—a form of corset—to improve their figure (very necessary when you remember Edwardian eating habits!) It was not unknown, either, for men to use cosmetics as a cheap substitute for expensive holiday bills. Max Beerbohm noted that artificial sun-tans were applied by 'countless gentlemen who walk about town in the time of its desertion from August to October, artificially bronzed,

The caricaturist Max Beerbohm, as he saw himself

quite knows where the lounge suit came from, but some people say it originated one day when a gentleman out riding grew rather impatient with his coat tails, which kept getting caught up, so he cut them off. The King liked the lounge suit style so much that he had it made up in checked tweeds for country and sporting wear. More conservative men around him began to wear lounge jackets with matching waistcoats and trousers in narrowly-striped dark grey cloth to go about their business. These were the first three-piece suits.

Most twentieth-century men's fashions have been borrowed from sports clothes. The cut-away morning coat took its shape from the classic shape of the riding coat. The Norfolk jacket was a traditional jacket worn for shooting and golf, but in the nineteen-hundreds men began to wear it simply for idling away their spare time in the country. The jacket was very different from all their other coats: it was tweedy and box-pleated with yoked shoulders and a belted waistband, and they would wear it over matching knickerbockers, golf stockings (or occasionally, gaiters), stout shoes and a tweed cap. Or they might wear a fancy tweed sports jacket with a half-belt, centre-back vent and patch pockets with their favourite old flannel trousers for messing around doing nothing in particular. There was even a coat called a 'riding lounge'—a sort of hacking jacket for a quiet morning's trot in the country. Gentlemen often changed into lightweight indoor jackets when they were at home; they also had special kid jackets for travelling.

For cricket, players wore a long-sleeved sweater with a polo-neck collar (even the name 'polo-neck' is borrowed from the sport of playing polo) which was later to become a V-neck, often with a band of colour around the neck and hem, according to your club or college. One young boy watching a cricket match in Edwardian times remembered seeing 'the men in white flannels, white boots, and wearing straw boaters, the women, also in white, with hourglass figures and hats like windmills; all white, or nearly white, save for

as though they were fresh from the moors or from the Solent. This, I conceive, is done for purely social reasons'.[11]

King Edward VII set the fashion for leaving one's bottom waistcoat button undone, a fashion which was almost certainly due to his love of good food. But he set other styles, too. He often wore a lounge suit on occasions when a formal frock coat would have been more correct, and soon his circle of friends was following his example. Nobody

the men's black socks that sometimes showed above their buckskin boots'.[12]

Even in the evening King Edward VII did not like having to be too stiff and starchy. Formal evening wear was supposed to be a dress coat (with tails) worn with matching trousers, a white waistcoat and white tie; however, in the United States and in France many fashionable men were wearing a 'dinner jacket' (known as a 'Tuxedo' in America and a 'Monte Carlo' in France). The King rather liked this single-breasted jacket, with its silk

Artists at work, wearing Norfolk jackets, knickerbockers and gaiters

lapels and informal, unbuttoned look, and he soon set the trend in Britain of wearing a dinner jacket with braided matching trousers, unless the occasion happened to be very formal, when, of course, he wore a dress coat.

The male equivalent of the tea-gown was the 'smoking jacket', which was worn informally in the evening. These jackets were made in beautiful dark silks and velvets and trimmed with frogging or cord. Men liked to wear them because they could easily be thrown over their everyday trousers, or worn formally with evening trousers, or even worn with matching velvet trousers and belted with a tasselled girdle. You have probably seen pictures of gentlemen smoking in their studies wearing smoking jackets and little velvet smoking caps trimmed with a long droopy tassel, in the Turkish style.

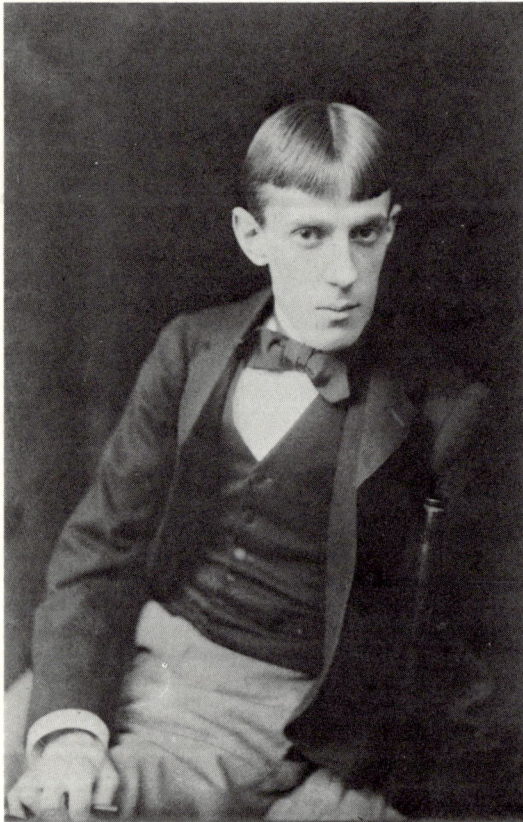

The artist Aubrey Beardsley, immaculately dressed in a dark coat and light trousers

In 1900 men were still wearing very high starched linen collars which look to us as if they were choking their wearers to death. People used to say, jokingly, that Prince Albert choked to death at an early age because of his unusually high wing collars! During the early years of the century softer, shorter collars became more acceptable, although the high, single wing collar was still worn with evening dress. If you could not afford to put on a freshly starched collar each day, you bought celluloid or even rubber collars which, the makers claimed, could be sponged clean. The Edwardians wore many different kinds of tie. The 'bow-tie' was usually only worn with a wing collar—that is, on very formal occasions. What we now think of as an ordinary tie was then called a 'four-in-hand' and had a square or pointed end. The 'Ascot' tie was twisted or tied once, rather like a cravat, with the ends held in place using a tie-pin or stud. Long thin ties were tied into a 'sailor's knot', that is, a reef knot with the ends hanging down rather like a cowboy's or a Teddy Boy's bootlace tie later. Many men sported their old school, club or regimental colours on their ties.

During the late nineteenth century 'modern' people took to wearing Dr Gustav Jaeger's new sanitary woollen clothing and combinations which were designed to be worn next to the skin. By the turn of the century wool underwear was generally accepted both among men and women, especially for sporting activities. It was said that when the playwright George Bernard Shaw went out for a country stroll wearing his full-length Jaeger outfit, the friction of his arms swinging against the woollen stockinet of his underwear made a chirping noise like a cricket so that his companions could hardly hear themselves speak! Edwardian gentlemen kept themselves very warm, with woollen combinations on the inside and heavy top coats on the outside. The most popular style of overcoat was the 'Chesterfield', a longer, heavier version of the classic overcoat worn nowadays. The 'Ulster' was a looser, even heavier coat, often with a cape or hood attached. The 'Inverness' cape

The Prince of Wales (later King Edward VII) wearing a Chesterfield coat

was made with two winged cape pieces above the sleeves; this is the style always worn by Sherlock Holmes as he darts through the November mists in pursuit of dangerous criminals!

No gentleman ever went out without a hat, and a well-dressed man would have an entire shelf devoted to hats for different occasions. He would be sure to have a top hat, which he would wear with his frock coat, morning coat, and evening dress. If he was a regular opera-goer, he might possess a 'Gibus'—an amazing silk hat with a collapsible spring inside, so that it could be folded up completely flat during the performance and placed under the theatre seat. In addition, he might wear any of the following: a bowler, a Homburg or trilby for smarter occasions; a deerstalker (shades of Sherlock Holmes again), maybe a 'wide awake' or perhaps a tweed golfing cap for less formal days. If he were lucky enough to go out on a summer day's jaunt, he would probably wear a boater (a flat straw hat) tipped at a rakish angle over his forehead. Underneath his hat, a gentleman's hair would be short and neatly trimmed, parted at the side or centre and kept tidily in place with lightly perfumed brilliantine or hair-cream. Most men had moustaches, but beards and side whiskers were regarded as not quite the thing, although all Victorian gentlemen had grown them.

Men's shoes became so long and pointed during the nineteen-hundreds that at one time they were known as 'tooth picks'. Black leather shoes were worn in town, brown leather in the country. Smart men no longer wore boots: they were becoming the trade-mark of the working man. When they were in evening dress, some men still wore old-fashioned low-cut black pumps trimmed with a flat black bow, but most preferred the newer patent leather lace-up shoes. Their socks were long, often silk, and were held up by sus-penders on a garter just below the knee. On wet days a smart gentleman, if he were forced to do a lot of walking, would slip a pair of galoshes over his shoes. These were of thin rubber and fitted tightly over the front and sole of the shoe and were held behind the heel by a buckle or an elastic band. At the seaside a man would wear a pair of the new canvas shoes with rubber soles to run over the shingle.

Oscar Wilde, author and playwright, sitting for the camera in frock coat and striped trousers

A gentleman's accessories were far more important then than they are now—they could make or mar his style of dress. He would always wear gloves, of either kid or doeskin, when he was in town; for dancing he would carry a pair of spanking white cotton gloves which he would button on when the time came to lead a lady on to the dance floor; when out cycling or walking he would wear thick leather gloves. No gentleman would emerge in public without a white silk, linen or cotton handkerchief tucked into his breast pocket. If the weather happened to be a little chilly he might wrap a fringed scarf of knitted silk or wool around his neck. He would wear beige, grey or white spats (short for 'spatter-dashes') on his feet to protect his shoes from dirt and mud at a time when road surfaces were still rough; he would button them up on one side of the foot and ankle, and they would be kept in place over the upper part of the shoes by a strap and buckle under the foot.

At the beginning of the century gentlemen still carried a cane or ebony stick mounted in silver, or even gold. Some of these sticks were so cleverly designed that you could carry inside them cigarettes, pipes, pencils or a small flask of brandy. On rainy days, the stick would be replaced by an elegant furled silk umbrella—but, if a gentleman were really stylish, he would travel everywhere by carriage or cab, and doormen carrying enormous umbrellas would rush out from the entrances of clubs and restaurants to escort him inside. A gentleman would always keep good time with a large pocket watch in his waistcoat pocket; wrist watches were virtually unknown in those days. His rings, tie-pins, studs and cuff-links would have been far more ornate than they are now. All in all, a distinguished Edwardian gentleman when formally dressed carried himself with an air of tremendous self-assurance, for in those days, when you could only look rightly or wrongly dressed (with no half measures), he was confident that he looked *correct*.

1. *The Graphic*, June 8, 1907
2. Lady Cynthia Asquith: *The Day Before Yesterday*, 1956
3. Lady Oxford, 1909
4. Ruby Miller: *Champagne for My Supper*
5. *The Lady*, 1902
6. Max Beerbohm: 'A Defence of Cosmetics', *The Yellow Book* Vol. 1, 1894
7. From 'Gentleman Joe', a musical comedy produced in 1895
8. Gwen Raverat: *Period Piece*, 1951
9. Ada Leverson: *Love's Shadow, The Little Ottleys*, 1908
10. Ellen Moers: *The Dandy*, 1960
11. Max Beerbohm: 'A Defence of Cosmetics', *The Yellow Book* Vol. 1, 1894
12. L. P. Hartley: *The Go Between*, 1953

Seen and Not Heard:
Children's Clothes 1900–1910

'The year 1900,' wrote one little late Victorian boy in his diary, 'had an almost mystical appeal to me; I could hardly wait for . . . the dawn of a Golden Age.'[1]

When you think how exciting the year 2000 sounds to us nowadays, you will understand what he meant. Unfortunately for children, life was far from being a Golden Age in Edwardian times._It is not surprising how solemn and much older than their age children looked in photographs, when you consider how they were treated. Their parents tended to look down upon them as small, unruly beings who should hardly be seen and

Everyday Edwardian children's clothes—an illustration from The Story of the Treasure Seekers, *by E. Nesbit*

The Royal children dressed in sailor outfits designed for cold weather

Playing blind man's buff at home

certainly not be heard, for they did not fit in with their parent's more formal way of life.

Although Victorian family life had included a growing interest in children's welfare, it was still felt that children would not learn anything unless they were given firm discipline to mould their characters. On the one side of the household there would probably be a strict, tyrannical father, on the other a helpless invalid mother who was constantly producing babies to make up the large family which was considered fashionable in those days. In middle-class families children were kept apart from their parents, were looked after by servants or a nurse (and as they grew up, a governess) and were only allowed to see their parents for a short time once or twice a day. Much of their childhood lives would have been spent being told what they must and must not do. Canings and slappings were an acceptable form of punishment in many homes. But, even if they were to be seen and not heard in the drawing-room, children could make their own entertainment tucked away at the top of the house in their nursery: dressing up, producing their own plays, stamp-collecting, catching and mounting butterflies, keeping pets or simply daydreaming over a book—and most people who grew up in such homes looked back at them with pleasure.

Poor children went to day school for a few years, or, if they managed to escape, they would kick a ball around the back streets. But neither rich nor poor children had the freedom to run about and play as most young people do nowadays. Their lives, like their clothes, were fussy and restricted.

Boys' clothes

At the turn of the century children's fashions were as greatly influenced by what the Royal children wore as they had been half a century earlier when King Edward VII was a little boy. One firm fashion trend which had lasted for years was the Highland dress which he wore at Balmoral Castle. Fashionable boys wore a jacket and waistcoat of braided velvet with a pleated tartan kilt over white drawers, tartan socks and shoes. To be really authentic they often added a sporran to complete the outfit, and perhaps a Scots hat.

The most popular style for both boys and girls was the naval look, which reflected the Royal family's associations with the Navy. If you had been walking through the streets in those days you would have seen children in miniature 'man o' war' suits, 'Jack Tar' suits with blouses, 'middy' (short for midshipman) suits with short jackets, double-breasted 'reefer' jackets sparkling with polished brass buttons and several other in-between variations of these sea-going styles. The sailor suit started off as a white summer suit for wearing at the seaside, but gradually it was adapted to be worn in winter, when it was made up in heavy navy-blue serge cloth, and was worn with a cap or Royal Tar hat with a wide curled-up brim to complete the outfit. If you look through old family photograph albums you will recognise the sailor suit by its open-necked blouse (always worn with a vest filling in the opening), its deep square collar at the back, and its matching bell-bottomed trousers or knee-length knickerbockers.

American fashions were introduced to European children because rich Americans were being accepted into King Edward's circle of friends. The 'American blouse' had a large turn-down, lace-trimmed collar, with falls of lace down the front of the blouse and around the wrists. With this blouse you would have worn your best knickerbockers or, if you were very grand, an elaborate velvet suit. This particular outfit became popular through the pages of Frances Hodgson-Burnett's famous children's book *Little Lord Fauntleroy*. In the chapter where the old English Earl first sets eyes on his American grandson, the author describes how he saw 'a graceful childish figure in a black velvet suit, with a lace collar, and with lovelocks waving about the handsome, manly little face, whose eyes met his with a look of innocent good-fellowship . . . rather like a small copy of the fairy prince'.[2] Many adults liked the idea of having children who looked and behaved like the 'manly' little

The Royal children at Abergeldie Castle in their Highland dress

A formal group of children in their 'Little Lord Fauntleroy' best

Lord Fauntleroy. Not only did they dress their sons in these impractical outfits; some parents encouraged their boys' hair to grow until it flowed around their shoulders in thick curls like Lord Fauntleroy's. No healthy, playful child could enjoy life dressed up in this way.

For most boys, however, Sunday best was an 'Eton suit' (named after the young boys' uniform worn at Eton College). This had a short round jacket with deep lapels and was worn either as a dress jacket over matching trousers, or as school uniform with a waistcoat and trousers of a lighter colour. Like their fathers, boys also wore Norfolk jackets. To begin with, these were a loose kind of shirt, pleated at the front and back and held with a sash, but gradually they began to follow the style of men's Norfolk jackets—they became tight, belted, with or without pleats, and were worn with matching tweed knickerbockers. One well-known writer who was a boy during Edwardian times recalls that in a photograph taken in 1900 he was 'wearing an Eton collar and a bow tie; a round Norfolk jacket cut very high across the chest, incised leather buttons, round as bullets, conscientiously done up, and a belt which I have drawn more tightly than I need have. My breeches were secured below the knee with a cloth strap and buckle, but these were hidden by thick black stockings, the garters of which, coming just below the straps, put a double strain on the circulation of my legs. To complete the picture, a pair of obviously new boots, looking larger for being new, and with the tabs, which I must have forgotten to tuck in, standing up boldly'.[3] Tabs were leather tags at the back of the boot which were used to pull up the heels.

30

The Royal children dressed in summer sailor suits

Both Etons and Norfolks were worn by older boys, particularly if they went away to school. Schoolboys, of course, made all sorts of interesting changes to their uniforms according to the traditions of their particular school. Stalky and his friends, the central characters of Rudyard Kipling's schoolboy book *Stalky & Co.*, wore 'the stiffest of stick-up collars, which custom decreed could be worn only by the Sixth . . . they crammed their caps at the extreme back of their heads, instead of a trifle over one eye as the Fifth should, and rejoiced in patent-leather boots on week-days, and marvellous made-up ties on Sundays'.[4] The flannel jackets with patch pockets which boys wore for cricket and school sports were known as 'blazers' and have since become a standard feature of twentieth-century schoolboy dress. Games clothes, apart from steadily becoming

briefer and more light-weight, have changed little. Any young football enthusiast nowadays would be able to picture an Edwardian player from Kipling's description of Stalky, 'playing substitute for the Old Boys, magnificent in black jersey, white knickers, and black stockings [long socks]'.[5]

Whatever the style of their jackets, boys always wore with them waistcoats in a matching cloth, done up with high V-necked fastenings. Underneath, their long shirts were very different from the shirts you wear now: they had a pleated front panel and sometimes a tab at the bottom, so that the shirt could be buttoned to their drawers, to stop all the various bits of clothing coming apart at the waist. Attached to the shirts with studs were narrow, uncomfortable stiff collars, either a turn-down style or else a single collar.

31

A small boy wearing high fashion: lace, tartan and a sailor hat!

Boys of your great-grandparents' day wore dark-coloured ribbed stockings with high-cut boots which laced up the front or buttoned down the side. No child, unless he was poor and scruffy, went out without a hat. It might be a low-crowned bowler, a sailor hat, a Scots hat or a close-fitting peaked cloth cap. Older boys wore rather grand top hats on more formal occasions and for Sunday best.

At about this time a few people were beginning to realise that children would be happier wearing looser, lighter clothes in summer. Rich boys whose parents could afford full outfits of summer-weight clothes as well as winter clothes were greatly envied. One little Edwardian boy practically baking to a frazzle in his thick clothes described his friend's summer outfit:

> He was wearing a light flannel suit. His shirt was not open but it was loose at the neck; his knickers could not be called shorts, for they came well below his knees but they also were loose, they flapped, they let the air in. Below them, not quite meeting them, he wore a pair of thin grey stockings neatly turned over their supporting garters; and on his feet—wonder of wonders—not boots but what then were called low shoes. To a lightly clad child of today this would seem thick winter wear; to me it might have been a bathing-suit, it looked so inadequate to the proper, serious function of clothes.'[6]

In cold weather, boys either wore their own style of overcoat, known as a 'paletot', or they imitated their fathers by wearing small Ulsters with belts or half-belts across the back and a hood or cape. Alternatively, they might possess a small-size Inverness cape. On bitterly cold days they might have worn a double-breasted reefer coat made from a cloth far thicker and rougher than that used for an ordinary reefer jacket. Heating was still somewhat primitive in those days, so really warm clothing was essential.

It was essential that summer clothes should become looser sooner or later: during the early years of the nineteen-hundreds your great-grandparents, in all their layers of clothing, experienced extraordinarily long, hot summers due to some freak weather.

For swimming at the seaside, boys would have worn jersey combination bathing suits. We would think these suits cumbersome now, but to Edwardian children they seemed a miracle, leaving legs and arms free to splash out, even though eventually the suit became rather heavy and unpleasant to wear, once it was waterlogged. At night, men and boys were beginning to wear pyjamas belted with a cord instead of the old-fashioned ankle-length night-shirt. This changeover was taking place at the time when Edith Nesbit was writing her book about *The Bastables*, the adventures of a family of fun-loving children:

Then we got into our pyjamas. It was Oswald who asked Father to let us have pyjamas instead of nightgowns; they are so convenient for dressing up when you wish to act clowns, or West Indian planters, or any loose-clothed characters.[7]

But apart from pyjamas, clothes were still designed more for show than for living. So thought one of the heroines of an Edwardian children's book, who tried counting the buttons on her brother's Sunday suit—she found *twenty-four* altogether!

Children paddling in their summer clothes at Yarmouth

Girls' clothes

Girls had an even harder time than boys. To begin with, their underclothes were almost as complicated as those of their mothers. And if that was not enough, at the age of fourteen a girl was forced to go into longer skirts and put up her hair—in effect, to become a dignified young lady, whether she liked the idea or not. One woman in 1935, looking back at her late Victorian childhood, thought how much children's clothes had improved in the intervening years:

> What I, on behalf of my fifty-years ago self most envy the little girls of today is the fewness and simplicity of their garments . . . We, too, put on first of all a vest. Then a chemise, a garment whose use was never apparent to us, but we were given to understand that it wouldn't be at all "nice" to go without it. It was made of calico and reached to the knees. Next "stays", a strip of wadded pique whose use was unmistakable. In addition to the five buttons that fastened our stays up the back, they had a number of other buttons at various levels and intervals round the waist. Two of these held up the elastic "spenders" of our stockings; the five buttonholes of our drawers belonged to the other three, and yet two more were buttoned into two holes in the band of our flannel petticoat. Over that came a white petticoat made with a bodice. The edges of all the white garments were decorated with rather scratchy cambric trimming . . . I have forgotten the stockings themselves, long black stockings reaching above the knee, woollen in winter, thick cotton in summer.[8]

There might be layers of flannel petticoat to be endured in winter, but lighter cotton was worn in summer. Petticoats were sometimes very dainty, however. One girl's best petticoat 'was white and soft and frilly, and trimmed with lace, and very, very pretty, quite as pretty as a frock, if not more so'.[9] And with so many layers, who was to notice if one or two petticoats were used for making into bandages, carrying things in, hiding things away and even sewing up to make a small tent? They 'really are very useful, especially when the band is cut off'[10] noted the hero of *The*

Wouldbegoods. With her scratchy thick stockings a girl would wear long boots laced or buttoned over the instep of her foot. But for best she would probably wear barred shoes or even low-fronted buckled shoes to go to formal tea parties, if she was a little older.

The sailor look was as popular for girls as it was for boys. With their sailor blouses, the collars trimmed with row upon row of navy or white cord, girls wore pleated skirts in navy serge or white drill. A magazine of the period described contemporary summer outfits like this:

> Next to the skin the child is to wear a thin woollen gauze combination, very short in the leg; over that a stay body to which is buttoned a pair of blue serge knickerbockers unlined. Over that only one skirt is worn and that has seven flat buttons sewn on the wrong side near the hem. On the upper part of the skirt are seven corresponding loops so that for paddling the desired shortness is easily attained by buttoning the bottom of the dress to the loops. A little blouse of white serge or washing silk is worn with the skirt and a short blue serge jacket added according to the weather or time of day . . . Long merino stockings should be worn, which should pass under the knickers. To take off the effect of the sun's rays on the head it is well to give the hat a complete green head lining, using a dull green so as to avoid arsenical dyes.[11]

By 1900 the jacket and skirt had become virtually a uniform for girls, worn under a full-length coat in the same style and reaching to just below the knee. At the seaside or in the country, however, girls were beginning to wear blazers of stripey flannel.

Perhaps the most important item of clothing at the turn of the century was the pinafore. It was the only garment designed to meet the practical needs of a child rather than merely copying the elaborate clothes worn by its parents. During the late nineteenth century the 'dress pinafore' of white muslin, trimmed with frills and lace insertions, was popular, for it protected the dress worn underneath and could be easily changed. From this another kind of pinafore developed

Girls in their best pinafores and sashes

Small girl dressed for the seaside in cotton drawers

—the 'frock pinafore', which came to be called a 'blouse'; it was a fairly loose garment, sashed or belted with a hook at the back, made of holland or cotton in summer, heavy alpaca or wool in winter. Smock dresses were also popular, and the pattern books of the time featured traditional country smocking designs which skilful seamstresses could apply to brighten up a plain smock. Young children who did not have much of a waistline found these styles (which hung down straight from a shoulder yoke) easy to wear. White and cream muslin or silk were the most popular colours for smocks, with perhaps a sash added in a pastel tone. Girls' hats were usually either sailor styles or tam-o'-shanters, held on with tight elastic under the chin, but for best a girl might wear something as amazing as one of her mother's creations:

> Anthea, who had had the misfortune to sit on her hat earlier in the day, wished to buy another. She chose a very beautiful one, trimmed in pink roses and the blue breasts of peacocks. It was marked in the window, 'Paris Model, three guineas'.[12]

Gloves were always worn out of doors with hats. Like their mothers, girls had long hair

Little girl wearing high fashion: flowers, frills, pleats and bows

which was tied back with all manner of ribbons and bows. But however neat and sweet they looked in their freshly starched pinafores with their hair neatly brushed, inevitably they felt irritated and uncomfortable in all the hot layers, tight lacing and endless buttons and hooks. One girl recalled very vividly a new dress bought at Peter Robinson:

> . . . the dress was a salmon pink surah with cream silk trimmings . . . it was some comfort to slip the pretty dress on over the stiff scratchy petticoats that were one of the minor tortures of

my life. So was the hat elastic which left a red mark under my chin and when slipped behind my ears for relief made my head ache. So were the tight little kid gloves, worked down my fingers, till I could get my thumb in. So were the bronze boots now being buttoned over two pairs of stockings, cashmere underneath and silk on top, so that I shouldn't take cold; because of this my insteps were pinched and my feet icy. But the dress did look nice . . .[13]

The Rational Dress Society, which had made so many practical suggestions for changing women's clothes, recommended many reforms for children's dress. They felt that children should wear more wool: woollen combinations; buttoned woollen stays; woollen stockings; divided skirts; and smock frocks. They also recommended what eventually became traditional girls' school uniform: a blouse worn underneath a pinafore dress.

Many children never wore any of these smart fashions. In large families, if parents could afford new children's clothes, they would be handed down one by one from the eldest child to the youngest, until they were worn out. But in very poor families the children never even saw new things. If they were lucky and lived in London, they might be given clothes donated to the East End missions by charitable ladies. Otherwise, their mothers would go to the rag markets held regularly in the poor areas of all big cities and buy second-hand, threadbare remnants which they would patch together for their children. It was certainly a case of one fashion for the rich, another for the poor.

1. L.P. Hartley: *The Go Between*, 1953
2. Frances Hodgson-Burnett: *Little Lord Fauntleroy*, 1886
3. L.P. Hartley: *The Go Between*, 1953
4. Rudyard Kipling: *Stalky & Co*, 1899
5. Rudyard Kipling: *Stalky & Co*, 1899
6. L.P. Hartley: *The Go Between*, 1953
7. Edith Nesbit: *Oswald Bastable & Others*, 1905
8. Eleanor Acland: *Goodbye for the Present*, 1935
9. Edith Nesbit: *Five Children and It*, 1902
10. Edith Nesbit: *The Wouldbegoods*, 1901
11. *The Housewife*, 1896
12. Edith Nesbit: *Five Children and It*, 1902
13. Eleanor Farjeon: *A Nursery in the Nineties*, 1935

Ragged backstreet children in London's East End

Ladies Breathe Again: 1908–1914

What is it about her clothes that makes a twentieth-century woman look modern? There are many obvious answers to this question, but perhaps more important than any of them is this: a modern woman's clothes follow her natural body shape. Of course, she may be a slave to fashion and wear wide gathered skirts one season, huge hats the next, and constantly be moving her waistline up and down; but she no longer distorts her shape with the artificial crinoline hoops or bustle backs of the past centuries. During the early nineteen-hundreds women's shapes were still being bent into strange unnatural lines by their S-shaped corsets, but in 1908 there was a great change. In May 1908 *Vogue* magazine reported:

> The fashionable figure is growing straighter and straighter, less bust, less hips, more waist, and a wonderfully long, slender suppleness about the limbs . . . the long skirt reveals plainly every line and curve of the leg from hip to ankle. The leg has suddenly become fashionable.[1]

The new corset, as advertised in 1911

At the time everyone thought this look was just the start of another seasonal fashion, but looking back we now realise that this was actually the beginning of twentieth-century fashion.

The man mainly responsible for uncovering women's natural body shape was the Paris *couturier* Paul Poiret, a great designer and showman. He had never liked the artificial lines of the S-shape; he preferred to design clothes for a straight figure shape with a lower bustline, a much looser waist and narrower, less rounded hips. In order to achieve the shape he wanted, he decided to make his gowns on a different kind of foundation. The corset that he designed started at a point well below the bust and reached right down almost to the knee, minimising instead of exaggerating its wearer's curves. Nowadays we would find his foundation horribly constricting, but

A dainty afternoon frock, 1909

to Edwardian women who had been used to the S-shaped corset, it was wonderfully comfortable. Its only disadvantage was its extreme length—sitting down became almost impossible, so very soon he had them made much shorter. Because these new corsets no longer pressed up under the bust, another bust support was needed, so first bodices, then brassières began to be worn. For the first time since the early nineteenth century women were able to stand upright in their foundation garments and move more easily (although *Punch* magazine thought women's shapes were still a little strange and that the new corset gave them

A figure like a seal reared up on end
And poking forward with a studied bend.[2]

Like all big fashion changes of the twentieth century, the new form of dress coincided with a gradual change in women's social position. Those women who were beginning to venture outside the home and to enter careers for the first time now needed clothes in which they could move quickly and work comfortably. A number of women both in Britain and in the United States (known as Suffragettes) were campaigning for the vote for women. They helped to bring the age of lace, pleats and flounces to an end—for how could women move around getting things done if they were continually hampered by unnecessary and dirt-catching tucks and frills? The same applied to all those petticoats and underclothes; they hindered movements and they spoiled the line of the new straighter-cut dresses. These new shapes had no room, either, for concealed pockets. Instead, women began to carry around their odds and ends in handbags.

Ladies still wore elaborate clothes to grand parties and formal gatherings; after all, clothes were even more of a status symbol in those days than they are now, when most people can afford to dress quite well. But in the years leading up to the First World War women tended to wear softer, more supple fabrics with a printed or woven pattern. Instead of all those sewn-on frills and flounces

The artiste Gaby Deslys wearing a hobble skirt decorated with tassels

the fashionable decoration was now a simple tassel. And skirts were now an inch or two shorter, to make walking easier.

Women still had a long way to go in their obstacle race towards a comfortable form of dress. Perhaps Paul Poiret had this in mind when he created a most extraordinary fashion: the 'hobble skirt'. This skirt looked, sideways on, like the trouser leg of a man's suit, and to keep the skirt looking narrow many fashionable women wore a small decorative band or strap round the skirt just above the hem, so that they could literally only hobble along! More active women wore their hobble skirts with flat pleats inserted near the hem, or they simply slit the sides or front so that they could walk more easily.

Paul Poiret's other entirely new fashion idea was the 'Turkish' or 'harem' skirt. Women achieved this exotic look by wearing baggy trousers, half-hidden under a tunic or overdress open at the sides and sometimes they wore divided skirts which separated at the knee. There was even one variation where the tunic hem contained a strand of wire running inside it, so that the bottom of the tunic stood away from the underskirt or trousers like a lampshade! Baggy trousers for women was a revolutionary idea, but the fashion did not catch on outside Paris—most women were not yet ready for them.

At about this time designers began to introduce startling new colours in their fashion collections instead of the previous pastel shades, which were now thought to be wishy-washy and out of date. In 1906 the Russian impresario Serge Diaghilev staged a gloriously colourful exhibition of Russian art in Paris; he followed up his success in 1909 by bringing the Ballets Russes to dance in the Châtelet Theatre in Paris, and in 1911 this ballet was brought over to dance in London by the conductor Sir Thomas Beecham, during the Coronation celebrations of King George V. Suddenly, everybody was talking about the ballet 'Schéhérezade'. Audiences thrilled to the brilliant dancing and high leaps of the Russian dancer Vaslav Nijinsky, and they adored the exotic costumes created for the dancers by Diaghilev's designer Leon Bakst. For his costumes Bakst used wild, Oriental colours: emerald greens, kingfisher blues, violet and magenta, orange, yellow and fuchsia pinks. There were turbans and tassels everywhere; and the simple, striking shapes of his costumes and sets caught the imaginations of fashionable people everywhere. Bakst was asked to design collections of daytime and evening wear for the fashion house of Paquin, and, not to be outdone, Poiret interpreted the new vibrant colours and styles in his own fashion collections.

While in Paris the fashionable world was flocking to be dressed by Poiret and Paquin, in London ladies were making their way to the House of Lucile to buy their gowns from Lady Duff-Gordon, who was then London's leading *couturière*. She produced exquisite and elegant clothes, but she was also sought after for her sheer originality. To begin with, she hated the shapeless white cotton and thick grey woollen Dr Jaeger underpinnings which English women considered the decent thing to wear beneath their clothes. So she made underclothes 'as delicate as cobwebs and as beautifully tinted as flowers, and half the women in London flocked to see them, though they had not the courage to buy them at first . . . But slowly one by one they slunk into the shop in a rather shame-faced way and departed carrying an inconspicuous parcel, which contained a crêpe de Chine or a chiffon petticoat, and although one or two returned to bring the new purchases sorrowfully back because a Victorian husband had "put his foot down", the majority came back to order more'.[3] Maison Lucile was much more than just a shop. Lady Duff-Gordon's dress collections were displayed in an elegant salon decorated in soft shades of grey; the invitations were printed on dainty cards as if she was holding a social party rather than a business promotion; she showed her model gowns on beautiful live mannequins, which was considered very daring at the time; and instead of calling her designs 'the green velvet' or 'the ivory satin' like other dressmakers, she gave them exotic faraway names such as 'When Passion's

As They are Worn: Results of Léo

Exotic turbans, patterns and shapes crea

Bakst's Creation of Modern Dresses.

BY PAUL MERAS.

Leon Bakst for the House of Poiret

Thrall is O'er', 'Do You Love Me?', 'Red Mouth of a Venomous Flower' and 'A Frenzied Song of Amorous Things'—all of which delighted her customers. All in all, she was doing what her fellow *couturiers* were doing in Paris—raising fashion away from the world of vulgar trade and into the elevated heights of aristocratic entertainment. Because she herself was a titled lady, famous rich women rushed to shop at her establishment; her customers included the Duchess of Westminster, Margot Asquith, Princess Alice and Ellen Terry, the famous English actress.

A new amusement was beginning to catch on at about this time: dancing. In 1907 Isadora Duncan, an American dancer who was also a very strong-minded woman, daringly performed on stage in Paris wearing ankle-length, flowing classical robes. She insisted on wearing her costume without

The latest fashion: a tango tea in London's West End

corsets or underwear (which she considered unhealthy) and danced barefoot to allow herself full freedom of movement. Another

well known dancer, Maud Allan, introduced a form of movement based on Grecian vase painting, and accompanied only by pipes and cymbals she danced around the stage wearing only a wisp of chiffon! On music-hall platforms dancers dressed and made up to look like Apaches and vampires were extremely popular. But the biggest craze of all which swept round the world in 1911 was the 'Tango'. Many people considered this wild, abandoned (for so it seemed to your great-grandparents at that time) South American dance vulgar and scandalous, but nevertheless it became the latest thing to hold what were known as *thés dansants* (tea dances) and tango parties. You could not possibly dance a light-hearted tango in an Edwardian tea-gown, but the new Poiret-style afternoon dresses or 'princess robes', with their elbow-length sleeves, slit up the sides above the ankle, were ideal. With your tango skirt you wore thin-soled shoes with cross-over ribbons up the leg. Following in the steps of the tango, dance after dance was introduced from America, with marvellous names such as the 'Turkey Trot', the 'Mexican Mix-up', the 'Chimpanzee Cuddle' and the 'Bunny Hug'. Many of these dances were made popular by Mr and Mrs Vernon Castle, an American husband and wife team who entertained with dance demonstrations in the new night-clubs springing up all over Europe and in the United States. Mrs Irene Castle became *the* fashion leader, for her slim boyish figure and style of dress were much admired. In 1913 she made newspaper headlines by having her hair cut in a 'bob'—a very short style that was soon to be copied by women everywhere. Along with the Castles, another American import into Europe was ragtime music. People began to listen to this new music at home on 'Victrolas', an early form of gramophone which you had to keep winding up by hand. It is not surprising that women's fashions became brighter and racier to match the exciting new world of music and dance many people were enjoying.

The newly invented motor car brought thrills and flurries of dust into many people's lives for the first time during the late nineteen-hundreds, when cars became more easily obtainable. You can feel for yourself the frenzy of those early days of motoring in this passage from *The Wind in the Willows*, when Mr Toad first sets eyes on a motor car:

> The 'poop-poop' rang with a brazen shout in their ears, they had a moment's glimpse of an interior of glittering plate-glass and rich morocco, and the magnificent motor-car, immense, breath-snatching, passionate, with its pilot tense and hugging his wheel, possessed all earth and air for the fraction of a second, flung an enveloping cloud of dust that blinded and enwrapped them utterly, and then dwindled to a speck in the far distance, changed back into a droning bee once more.[4]

This description explains exactly why such complicated clothes (the author called them 'those singularly hideous habiliments') were necessary for motoring: it was an extremely messy, if enjoyable, activity. When Mr Toad sets out in his brand-new motor car he swaggers down the steps of Toad Hall drawing on his gauntleted gloves, 'arrayed in goggles, cap, gaiters, and enormous overcoat'. In those days ladies had to take great care to protect their delicate pale complexions, their fine hair and their soft hands from the great clouds of dust raised on the country roads where they drove, for as yet few roads had the smooth macadam surface which we take for granted nowadays. In winter, a lady was advised to wear over her indoor clothes a waterproof top-coat lined with chamois leather and fur which she would wrap well around her legs, while her face was wrapped in a grey Shetland veil two yards long and threequarters of a yard wide which, if necessary, she would pull right across her face over her ugly, thick motoring goggles. In addition, she might wear a wide, flat tweed

Mr Toad in his motoring outfit

45

cap to show that she was a motorist. French fashion magazines even showed pet dogs wearing motoring goggles and dust coats as they sat on their owners' laps! You can imagine what a hindrance all these clothes could be. Sometimes they were actually dangerous: the dancer Isadora Duncan caught the trailing end of the protective gauze veil she was wearing in the spokes of her motor car while driving and was immediately choked to death.

Swimming was another very popular sport. Around the year 1910 it became acceptable to wear a one-piece suit in serge or woven wool instead of the many layers previously considered decent. The champion American swimmer, Annette Kellerman, had pioneered the one-piece style back in 1900.

As the high-waisted, straight-sided Empire line became the fashionable style of dress, dressmakers tried to soften the line with draped cross-over bodices and tunic tops. To go with this looser, flowing line, little V-necks were introduced into blouses and dresses. At first church authorities cried out against them as being immoral. But by 1912 what *Punch* called the 'pneumonia blouse' was very popular, even if it was sometimes worn with a 'fill-in' for modesty's sake. Alternatively, a round neck with a Peter Pan collar was worn. These lower necks were thought to be healthier than the high boned collars of earlier years. Magazines suggested that to repair the 'damage' caused by high stiff collars women should scrub their necks with hot water and soap, followed by applications of iced water to tone up their skin, finishing with a layer of skin-food and a bandage of cotton gauze soaked in lavender water!

Tailor-mades were now called 'costumes'. The coat part was often cut away over the stomach like a man's morning coat and fastened with buttons, while its sleeves might be cut in a baggier style than before. Evening dresses were now tube-like, usually a knee-length tunic worn over a floating gauze underskirt edged with bands of satin, velvet or brocade silk. Sashes were to be seen everywhere and the most common form of decora-

Annette Kellerman setting out to swim the Channel in her revolutionary one-piece suit

tion was heavy beaded embroidery. One especially beautiful dress of 1911 still preserved in a museum in Manchester is described thus:

> Pink and blue shot and watered silk with pink and blue gauze tunic. Embroidered net and appliqué lace trimmings to bodice, sleeves and hem of tunic. Bodice cross-over V neck with fill-in, elbow sleeves, narrow cord girdle, high waistline. Skirt straight and narrow, the back section overlapping tunic and falling to form a square train.[5]

Coats became rather splendid in the years just before the First World War. Perhaps this was because for the first time wealthy women were choosing to walk about from store to new department store to do their shopping, instead of taking a carriage everywhere, and therefore

COATS AND WRAPS.

"MILLICENT."
Charming Wrap of Floral Ninon, in Dainty Colourings, mounted over Cream Satin, suitable for smart Afternoon or Evening wear.
Price £2 18 6

"ADRIENNE."
Dainty Wrap, suitable for Day or Evening wear, of softest Moiré Bengaline, in the newest shade of Grey, lined Yellow Chiffon. Original and becoming Collar of Floral Printed Crêpe-de-Chine and Grey Satin.
Price £8 8 0

"MANON."
A Smart Unlined Wrap, suitable for Afternoon or Evening wear, in Moiré Bengaline.
Price £3 5 0

Carriage is paid on all Drapery Goods sent anywhere in the United Kingdom.

Winter coats as advertised by Marshall & Snelgrove

needed warmer top-coats to protect them from the elements. Or perhaps it was the influence of the Russian Ballet with its

Cossack furs. Whatever the reason, now that women's shapes were no longer squeezed in at the waist, they looked most imposing in their stylish coats with their bold lapels and collars. These coats were now made in heavy tweeds, sometimes fur-lined and sometimes made entirely of fur. Smart oilskin raincoats were now worn on rainy days; and advertisements for the famous Burberry raincoat stated that the coat combined 'the body warming powers of an ulster and the distinctive appearance of a smart overcoat for formal occasions'.

The enormous cartwheel hats of the early Edwardian era were now a thing of the past. Women now wore smaller, neater hats— beaver or plush tam-o'-shanters and berets pulled well down over the eyes, which were more in keeping with the new, slimmed-down silhouette. Paul Poiret and the House of

MILLINERY DEPARTMENT.

Elegant hats worn just before the outbreak of war

Paquin introduced exotic little turbans and elegant toques trimmed with osprey or ostrich feathers to complement their oriental designs. Little by little, women's hairstyles became smaller and neater, too; hair was now loosely waved and coiled into a bun at the back of the neck, or tied up at the back of the head in the evening. Women were now carrying bags of every description: Dorothy bags, which you closed with a drawstring and loops: shoulder bags on long cords; and silver chain bags. Ladies wore huge muffs and long fur stoles, dangling animal heads, tails and paws from their shoulders. And, as if that were not enough, it became fashionable to carry an umbrella in a shade to harmonise with your outfit; soon these grew so long and slender that eventually they were nearly shoulder-high from the ground! Smartest of all was the lady who carried a toy-sized dog wearing a bow to match her own outfit.

Children's clothes: 1911–1914

Schools were beginning to modernise school uniforms on the lines laid down earlier by the Rational Dress Society. Gym tunics, known as 'drill-dresses', came into general wear at about this time—and even today, girls in many schools wear a modern form of gymslip in an easy-care fabric with a blouse underneath. Like their mothers, girls were beginning to want to do the things that boys did. In 1909 Lord Baden-Powell founded the Girl Guide movement for those girls who envied their brothers in the Boy Scout organisation. The first uniform designed for the Girl Guides, was described like this:

Jersey of company colour.
Neckerchief of company colour.
Skirt, knickers, stockings dark blue.
Cap red biretta [a square cap], or in summer large straw hat.
Cape hooked up at the back.
Shoulder knot of the group colour on left shoulder.
Badges much the same as Boy Scouts.[6]

This was thought to be a very modern and practical outfit at the time.

The first Girl Guides in their uniforms

Apart from school and other uniforms, however, girls' clothes remained rather impractical. Smock dresses continued to be worn for a while, then, for no particular reason, the waistlines on children's dresses (including boys' tunic-tops) dropped right down to thigh-level, as their mother's waistlines were to do during the nineteen-twenties. One woman who remembered wearing low-belted dresses in her childhood recalled:

These dresses were not very comfortable, for often when running or jumping—or sometimes even when sitting down—the tight belt would suddenly split with the strain. Or else, if you had not been too careful in putting the belt through its slots, you would find yourself walking along with the belt round your ankles.[7]

But underclothes, at least, were becoming easier to wear. Stays, suspenders and stockings were dying out and many fashionable children were wearing threequarter-length socks, except for older girls, who still wore stockings. Like their parents, children began to wear clothes in more exciting colours, often edged with embroidery, which made a change from the rather monotonous navy-blue, white and sludgy tweeds of the previous years. Gradually, their lives were becoming brighter.

1. *Vogue* magazine, May 1908
2. From the verse entitled 'A Directoire Frock', *Punch*, 1909
3. Lady Duff-Gordon: *Discretions and Indiscretions*, 1932
4. Kenneth Grahame: *The Wind in the Willows*, 1908
5. Exhibit in the Gallery of English Costume, Manchester
6. Colonel R.S.S. Baden-Powell: *The Scheme for Girl Guides*, 1909
7. Iris Brooke: *English Children's Costume since 1775*

An early school lacrosse team in their gymslips

English boy's summer clothes worn in the West Indies

Chic little Parisian girls in their Sunday best

going to a brothel

Grey flannel, jerseys and embroidered smocks worn by children of all ages

Come, Dance Before the Music Stops: the 1914–18 War and the Nineteen-Twenties

When the world went to war in 1914 everyone thought peace would come again very soon. Initially it was a man's war. Women sat at home as they had always done, knitting and sewing little comforts such as mittens and scarves to boost the morale of the troops. Those few women who tried to offer their services to the war effort were politely but firmly refused, for it was thought that a woman's place in troubled times was waiting patiently to soothe and inspire the tired soldier when he came home on leave. One or two bolder women took no notice of what they were told to do. One of them, Dorothy Lawrence, disguised herself in a private's uniform and was smuggled to the Front, where she worked beside the engineers laying mines, until she was found out and sent home. Another determined woman, Flora Sandes, the daughter of a Suffolk vicar, fought alongside a Serbian regiment in full man's uniform and eventually was awarded the highest honour in the Serbian army. But for most women 1914 and the early part of 1915 were much like the pre-war years: their stay-at-home life and the clothes they wore to maintain that lifestyle remained much as before.

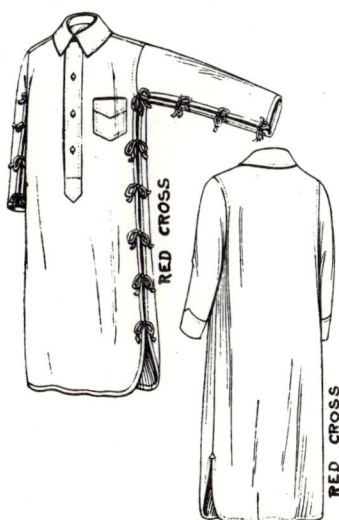

6270—Men's or Boys' Sack Night-Shirt. 132—Red Cross Convalescent Robe. 131—Red Cross Night-Shirt.

Butterick pattern advertising clothes to make for wounded soldiers

In 1915, fashion's tight tube-shaped gowns and hobble-skirts disappeared. They were replaced by wide-skirted, loose-belted tunics which only just skimmed the ankle, or by 'coat frocks'—high-waisted, belted dresses with straight pleated skirts and vast pockets gaping out at the sides, made in cotton or silk for summer and woollen cloth for winter wear. The reason for this sudden change was that at last women were called upon to do active war work; so many men were being sent to the Front to replace the enormous numbers killed by the monstrous new forms of modern warfare that the Government needed vast numbers of able-bodied people to keep the essential services running—and the only people available to do this work were women. Women drove vans, trams and ambulances, collected refuse, cleaned windows, manned railway signal boxes and collected tickets, swept chimneys, served in the police force and worked on the land. The Women's Army Auxiliary Corps, known as WAAC for short, served in Britain and abroad with the men's forces as cooks, clerks, drivers, mechanics and waitresses; later still the Women's Royal Naval Service and the Women's Royal Air Force were founded. The uniform designed for the WAAC—a belted khaki frock-coat—was very much like the more fashionable clothes worn by civilian women during the war years. Its shapeless 'barrel' outline and plain uncluttered look allowed women to go uncorseted and proclaimed to the world that women now had more important things to think about than just frills and feathers. The 23,000 servicewomen of the Women's Land Army, which was formed to produce more home-grown crops in 1917, when food was running short, went to work in sweaters, smocks, boots, round felt hats—and breeches. And by 1917 there were 700,000 women working in munitions factories producing weapons, shells, fuses and trench warfare supplies. They wore protective tunics and peg-top trousers, with their short bobbed hair tucked away under small caps, but they brightened up these dingy utility clothes with bright scarves and patterned blouses.

The rather shapeless dress styles favoured in 1916

52

Fortunately, there were few restrictions on fabrics during the First World War, except for a wool shortage in 1918, so women could dress in more traditional pretty tea-frocks and tea-coats in their off-duty moments. They even wore what they called 'semi-evening dress' at night when the occasion demanded. The House of Lucile was still producing the most sought-after gowns in London and New York during the Great War, but if you could not afford her luxury clothes, you would probably buy a ready-made dress from one of the new department stores. There were not likely to be sizing problems, for the loose shapeless styles of the war years fitted practically anybody. More and more women wanted to buy off-the-peg clothes, for they were now earning good wages compared with women's meagre earnings before the war. War workers could even afford modest fur coats—after all, they were the first modern working women of the twentieth century.

When the war ended in 1918, clothing manufacturers began to apply the new mass-production techniques they had developed during the war to making more fashionable, inexpensive civilian clothes. In America, scientists developed a new, artificial fibre and the 'washing frocks' made from the 'artificial silk' or 'rayon' (as it was called) could actually be washed over and over again. And now that a new type of iron—an electric one—was coming into general use, clothes could be pressed more safely and efficiently than ever before.

In 1918 the Government at last recognised that women were capable of being as able and conscientious as men: women over the age of thirty were given the vote and full rights of citizenship—but women did not obtain equal rights with men until 1928, when all women over twenty-one were able to vote. The large numbers of working women greatly enjoyed their new sense of freedom, earning good wage packets in the civilian jobs they had found once the war was over. Some of these women came to be known as 'flappers' because of the high-spirited way they dashed around enjoying themselves in the evenings and at weekends. The wealthier young women who spent their time indulging in wild parties and high living were called the 'Bright Young Things' by the newspaper gossip columnists who recorded their adventures. Bright Young Things liked to 'gate-crash' parties—the more original the party, the better. Perhaps the most extraordinary entertainment of the nineteen-twenties was a Baby Party, where men and women dressed up in baby clothes and ran races with perambulators (prams) round a very respectable (and very disapproving) London square. Out in the countryside, all-night treasure hunts became the rage. Women's lives were much gayer now, for after the hurly-burly of the war no-one wanted to bother themselves looking after modern young girls, so chaperones became a thing of the past. Young women felt free to go to night clubs and parties with their current boyfriend, as well as with friends.

Many women had little hope of marriage as a future. So many young men had been killed during the Great War that the surplus single women and widows realised they would have to support themselves for the rest of their lives. They were living like men, and they tried to look as manly, or as boyish, as possible. They went to great lengths to disguise their figures. To achieve the straight-up-and-down look a woman would always be dieting, and wore a brassière to flatten her bosom instead of supporting it, while round her hips she wore a straight-sided corset. Although skirt lengths went up, down, and into zig-zags throughout the nineteen-twenties, the bustless, waistless, hipless shape with a belt at hip level remained the fashionable look. The 'Twenties' look was above all sporty, made up of plain, light colours and easy-to-wear styles, for all those women who wanted to move freely and live brighter, healthier lives. Fashion writers announced early on: 'the ultra-modern woman wears only two types of clothes in the summer: sports things all day, and dance frocks all night!' When the professional tennis champion Suzanne Lenglen appeared on a court in 1919 wearing a calf-length, short-sleeved dress simply tied at the waist and with a cardigan thrown casually over her shoulder, she set the trend for brief, sporty clothes which we still follow today.

The Bright Young Things used to lounge around lazily one minute, the next they would be feverish with excitement and enthusiasm for the latest craze. One Young Thing wrote these lines, which seem to sum up the mood of the Twenties:

> Mother's advice, and father's fears,
> Alike are voted just a bore,
> There's negro music in our ears,
> The World is one huge dancing floor,
> We mean to tread the Primrose Path
> In spite of Mr Joynson-Hicks,*
> We're People of the Aftermath,
> We're girls of 1926.
>
> In greedy haste on pleasure bent,
> We have no time to think or feel,
> What need is there for sentiment,
> Now we've invented Sex-Appeal?
> We've silken legs and scarlet lips,
> We're young and hungry, wild and free,
> Our waists are round about the hips,
> Our skirts are well above the knee.
>
> We've boyish busts and Eton crops,
> We quiver to the saxophone,
> Come, dance before the music stops,
> And who can bear to be alone?
> Come, drink your gin, or miff your "snow",
> Since Youth is brief, and Love has wings,
> And Time will tarnish, 'ere we know,
> The brightness of the Bright Young Things.[1]

(*William Joynson-Hicks was a Home Secretary well-known for his strong disapproval of young people's morals during the Twenties.) Another writer, Noel Coward, caught the image of the time in his popular musical comedies; his male leading characters were always pictured speaking brittle, throwaway lines as they stood about in silk dressing-gowns, their hair slicked back, trailing long cigarette holders.

The Bright Young Things were always looking for new amusements. First, they fell in love with everything Egyptian, following the discovery of Tutankhamun's tomb. Then they became amateur psychoanalysts, trying to lay bare each other's innermost thoughts, and all because the psychologist Sigmund Freud's writings had just been published. They played with pogo sticks, then took to crossword puzzles, then to Chinese Mah-Jong, as one by one these new games became all the rage. But more exciting than any of these interests were the Hollywood silent films; everyone paid their sixpence entrance money to go to the 'picture-palace' (commonly known as the 'fleapit' or 'bug-hut') once or twice a week to see Charlie Chaplin, Rudolf Valentino playing in *The Sheik*, Douglas Fairbanks as a swashbuckling pirate or Mary Pickford as a little-girl-lost. Young Things wanted to look like the Screen Queens. For a while they made themselves look vampish and fascinating, whitening their skins, shadowing their eyes and painting their lips blood-red to look like the dangerous *femme fatale* stars Theda Bara and the 'It' girl Clara Bow. Then they copied the innocent-looking darlings Mary Pickford and Gladys Cooper, plucking their eyebrows until they achieved a high, thin, astonished look, varnishing their nails and darkening their lips into a 'Cupid's bow'. Everyone wore cosmetics openly now: in 1929 even the staid *Ladies Home Journal* wrote about one brand of lipstick, 'the alluring note of scarlet will stay with you all hours'. As for your hair, it was not enough just to have it bobbed; you had to have it 'shingled', too—cut really short at the back, then brought forward over the cheeks in 'kiss-curls'. In 1926 a few daring women had their cut chopped as short as a schoolboy's. This style, worn with a side parting and long dangly earrings, was called the 'Eton crop'.

In 1922 the British Broadcasting Corporation started to send out programmes from Marconi House in London over the wireless, and soon nearly every school-boy knew how to put together a crude 'crystal set' to pick up the transmissions. Jazz was the other sound craze of the Twenties. In 1919 the Dixieland Jazz Band came over to Europe from New Orleans and played in London for the first time, introducing listeners to numbers such as 'I'm Forever Blowing Bubbles', 'Alice Blue Gown' and 'Tiger Rag'. The Bright Young Things went wild about the new musicians, calling them 'divine', 'super' and 'king', and soon there was little to be heard but jazz, jazz, jazz, wherever you went. The Dixieland Jazz Band and the success of a new review called 'The Blackbirds', with its hit song 'Bye Bye Blackbird' suddenly made negroes and Harlem culture fashionable. It was because of this exciting new music that people refer to these years as 'The Jazz Age' and 'The Roaring Twenties'.

Film star Gladys Cooper wearing a baggy knitted jumper, 1920

Everyone who was anyone trailed a cloud of cigarette smoke behind them from a long holder. Every fashionable woman smoked, whereas only a few years before the very idea would have been frowned on. The 'cocktail hour' arrived from America and people began to drink potent alcoholic mixtures with saucy names like 'Widow's Kiss' and 'Maiden's Blush'. A new word was invented to describe the awful effects of over-drinking—'hangover' —and everyone joked about it (but few people joked about the Young Things who went a step further in their intoxicating experiments and became miserable drug addicts). Most evenings, after enjoying the latest West End revue, fashion-conscious Bright Young Things would go on to a nightclub, perhaps to the 'Midnight Follies' at the Hotel Metropole, or to have dinner and watch the 'Piccadilly Revels' at the Piccadilly Hotel, or simply head for the Trocadero. Here they jumped around and learnt the latest dances: the 'Foxtrot' in 1922, the slow uneasy 'Blues' in 1923, but above all the 'Charleston' which hit Europe in 1926. Everyone wanted to dance like the stylish American partners Fred and Adele Astaire. Professional male dancing partners known as 'gigolos' or 'lounge lizards' were employed by clubs and hotels to be hired out for dancing by rich unaccompanied women (there were many of these, with so many young men dead after the war). These professional partners were usually Latin American or Southern European and quite good-looking in a swarthy kind of way. Their clothes were 'tailored to swooning point with padded shoulders and mermaid hips', as one observer noted!

Back in the home, knitting needles were clicking furiously. Everyone, whatever their age, had taken their turn to knit for the troops during the war. Now women began to knit jumpers for themselves—long shapeless, wide-sleeved, V-necked woollen tubes which they wore pulled well down over their hips. Artificial silk yarn was nearly as popular as wool, for with it you could get the heavy, drooping effect which was all the rage then. You could also knit sleeveless lacy see-through

Negro musicians, ragtime and backless chiffon—all the ingredients of the Jazz Age

Fashionable knitwear adorned with Cubist designs

tops to wear over dresses, or put together a matching jumper and cardigan to wear as a 'twin-set'.

During the Twenties the *couture* houses of Paris began to dominate fashion more than ever before. The *couturière* Gabrielle Chanel was to be a fashion leader for the next thirty years, but her ideas influenced people most during the Twenties. She designed straight-cut clothes: her wool suits with their cardigan jackets and plain or pleated skirts were comfortable and easy to move in. But they were deceptively simple, for she designed for rich women who wanted to dress simply, but who wanted perfection in every detail. Chanel had jersey fabrics specially woven for her suits, usually in shades of grey and beige; then she would line them with fine silks, edge them with luxurious braiding and trim them with exquisite buttons. With her own clothes

(designed by herself, of course,) she wore fabulous chunky jewellery—enormous emeralds and rubies—but she realised that many women could not afford such incredibly expensive pieces, so she designed for her customers fake necklaces, bracelets, lapel-pins, brooches and earrings which were proudly referred to as 'costume jewellery'. Chanel, known by everyone as 'Coco', was the first designer to launch the sweater line (an idea which she borrowed from the 'Apache' street gangs of Paris), the pleated skirt, fake pearls, triangular scarves, Chanel No. 5 perfume, sling-back shoes and charm bracelets—all things that fashion-conscious women take for granted nowadays. Another Parisian designer, Jean Patou, was famous for his sporty clothes (he designed the outfit for Suzanne Lenglen which was so ahead of its time) and for his drifting chiffon cocktail

A lady perfectly dressed for Ascot by Captain Molyneux

dresses. The *couturière* Jeanne Lanvin produced some pretty 'picture frocks' in colours such as 'Lanvin blue' for her own daughter, and they became so sought-after by grown-up women who saw them that she adapted them for her lady customers. In England, anyone who was anyone went to the designer Captain Molyneux for her gowns. For women who wanted Paris styles—but not Paris prices—the department stores in London and other cities made their own copies of Paris fashions and took care to advertise them as 'Direct from Paris', for the very name conjured up a magic image of chic, style and elegance.

Perhaps the most startling thing about fashion in the Twenties is that women wore so few, and such brief clothes. You would think that having worn so many clothes for so long, most women would be catching colds and influenza all the time in their thin outfits, but they seem to have survived and, if anything, to have thrived. Their straight dresses either had long sleeves or no sleeves at all. In 1923 hemlines were eight inches from the ground and skirts were sometimes padded on the inside around the hips to make them look wider; in 1926 skirts rose to sixteen inches from the ground (knee-length) and by 1927 evening underskirts were as short as eighteen inches from the ground, although at this stage they were partially covered by drooping handkerchief-corner hems. Clergymen all over the world delivered sermons saying that short skirts were the work of the devil, and the Archbishop of Naples even claimed that the recent earthquake at Amalfi was due to God's anger on seeing such indecent garments! But from 1927 onwards skirt lengths gradually fell and at the same time women's waistlines rose to a more natural position.

Instead of tea-gowns, women now wore flimsy cocktail dresses held up by thin shoulder-straps. They were now exposing large expanses of back, so much so that one writer warned:

Lady, a word—but oh, beware!
   And prithee do not slight it—
If you will have your back so bare,
   Someone is sure to bite it.[2]

During the day jumper suits, jumpers-and-skirts and blouses-and-skirts of the kind made famous by Chanel, held with a hip-band or belt, were generally worn. They were decorated with a little beading or embroidery, a floating scarf, a draped sash, a large bow on one side of the hip, or worn with long strings of beads, slave bangles and drop earrings. As early as 1921 fashion magazines were advising:

> Dresses will be set off around the hips by beads, jet, and exquisitely worked motifs. Fringes are still in favour, and for the time being they will have to be in nothing but chenille [the fringing used to trim furniture upholstery], although on evening dresses they will mingle with other fringes of silver and crystals. Great gagalite buttons, as big as the brim of a tea-cup, are now put on mantles of woollen material and also on waistbands for morning wear, while evening dresses are adorned with mother-of-pearl motifs, chiselled like pieces of jewelry.[3]

Over their costumes or dresses women wore loose top-coats fastened with a single button at hip level, often with enormous fur collars. Their evening coats were often gorgeously embroidered with oriental patterns and had large, lavishly trimmed sleeves. The hat worn with everything was called a 'cloche', (a French word meaning 'bell'—which was exactly the shape of these hats). They had a high crown and a very narrow turned-up brim; you pulled them right down over your forehead until they almost covered your eyes. You might even pin a long feather on your cloche which would trail downwards over your shoulders—then you would look the cat's whiskers! And you probably would be carrying a dumpy, rather ugly umbrella tucked under your arm.

Now that land-girls and munition workers had taken the lead in wearing trousers, they were no longer such a shocking sight. All the same, they were only worn casually at home or on the beach. Fashionable women wore silk pyjamas, crêpe de Chine 'smoking suits' or brocade Turkish trouser suits rather as their mothers had worn tea-gowns—for lounging around in the evening. On the beach they

Mannishly-dressed woman with a cloche hat

often wore wide-legged beach pyjamas in a patterned silk or cotton over their bathing suits. And a few pairs of floppy trousers with turn-ups were to be seen on the tennis courts in the late Twenties.

Not only did people try to spend more time in the open air; they wanted to *look* as if they did, so women as well as men began to expose their skin out of doors and sunbathe when they could. Some people say that 'Coco' Chanel was the first woman to make a suntan look stylish, when she returned from a yachting holiday one afternoon wearing a spanking white suit and a dark golden tan. From then on, those who could afford it travelled to millionaires' playgrounds in sunny California and on the French Riviera, to parade in their brief bathing suits, billowing beach robes and razzmatazz pyjamas along the promenades.

By now the days of unnecessary underwear were gone and slim, fashionable women wore

Beautiful lingerie: a slip, nightgown and boudoir cap

a short slip and brief drawers or camiknickers (a slip and drawers combined). In the bedroom they wore beautifully embroidered dressing-gowns and boudoir caps. The Twenties were years of beautiful lingerie. One fashion writer wrote ecstatically in 1924:

> These garments—brief, filmy, flexible as the body itself—are few in quantity, exquisite in quality, and, out of respect to the natural lines of figures today, reminiscent of the classic robes of Artemis or Aphrodite, the lovely goddesses of antiquity . . . Ah, this new lingerie, a modern revelation, an airy, fairy gossamer, a garment conducive to the freedom of movement, mind, and matter, that has captivated femininity![4]

Artificial silk stockings, as well as silk and lisle, were now worn by all women. They were decorated with 'clocking', a design woven into the stocking up the outer side of each ankle; this was thought to be most flattering to the shape of the leg. Except for the seam up the back of each leg, it now looked as though all women were bare-legged in their flesh-coloured hosiery, and this shocked puritan clergymen almost as much as short skirts had done.

Considering that legs were on show now as they had never been before, there was not much variety in the shoes women wore. If you look at old photographs, the women are nearly always wearing a shoe with 'lavatory pedestal' heels and one or more bars across the instep, or else a lace-up pointed-toe brogue. Shoes were brown for the country, black for town and dyed to match one's evening gown after dark. In the slushy wintry weather of 1924 'Russian boots' were suddenly the rage: they were almost knee-length and they were the first items of clothing to be fastened with a new invention called a 'zip'!

Everyone who lived through the Twenties remembers the distinctive colours of the age: lacquer red; *eau-de-Nil* (named after the green waters of the Nile); pink; faded mastic yellow; but above all beige, in all its shades of almond, ivory, rose-beige, sand and Sahara khaki reminiscent of the war years. If you had been living then, you would have seen these colours echoed over and over again not only in clothes shops, but also in furnishings, house-paint, posters and the jazzy new 'art deco' designs to be seen adorning everything from tea-pots to cinemas.

Men's clothes

The Bright Young Men who escorted their 'flapper' girlfriends about in fast cars from tea-dances to roadhouse cafés wore their clothes with a much jauntier air than their fathers. Their summer 'uniform' was the boater and blazer look: a straw, flat-crowned, flat-brimmed hat with a striped band around it in old school or club colours, worn with a blazer, also in college stripes or with a club crest on the breast pocket, and cream flannel trousers. In 1925 men developed their own crazy fashion—the fashionable width for trouser legs became wider and wider until soon Oxford undergraduates were seen out walking in thirty-two-inch-wide trousers! But this fashion was finished almost as soon as it had begun, for it was not very practical.

A swell, with his monocle, silver-tipped cane and Oxford bags, 1925

The Prince of Wales (later King Edward VIII) dressed for golf in a check cap and Fair Isle V-necked jersey

Young 'swells' (dashing young men) up at Oxford and in London were often the dandies of the time. The writer Evelyn Waugh recalled one very smart undergraduate of the Twenties:

> He was tall, slim, rather swarthy, with large saucy eyes. The rest of us wore rough tweeds and brogues. He had on a smooth chocolate-brown suit with loud white stripes, suède shoes, a large bow-tie and he drew off yellow, wash-leather gloves as he came into the room.[5]

The Prince of Wales (who was to become King Edward VIII briefly before he abdicated from the Throne in 1936) was a great men's trend-setter. He liked to play golf in baggy plus-fours of Harris tweed worn with patterned Fair Isle sweaters, Argyle socks (with a diagonal check pattern), co-respondent ('two-tone') shoes and a large flat tweed cap; soon golf-players everywhere were wearing this cheerfully coloured outfit. The Prince of Wales did much to brighten up men's drab clothes, for he also liked to wear suède shoes, wide-knotted ties (people called this new, bold knot the 'Windsor tie'), and a navy dinner jacket instead of formal black evening wear. Men were quick to follow his comfortable example of wearing a soft shirt rather than the old-style stiff starchy one. After all, women were wearing more relaxed clothes, so why shouldn't they, too?

Children's clothes

In the early Twenties, people suddenly sat up and took a new look at their children. Parents began to realise that they had neglected their sons and daughters. They listened to the child specialists who said children were not evil little beings who could only learn things parrot-fashion under strict parental discipline; they were as individual as grown-ups and should be cherished and encouraged to learn things for themselves. One Twenties writer actually felt she had to spell out children's likes and dislikes to her readers—as if she was describing the habits of a new, unknown creature:

> Healthy Children like—
> A certain amount of freedom.
> Bodily activity—swimming, climbing, rowing, running. These things may cause you slight anxiety and inconvenience, but if you forbid them you arrest the growth of your child's mind as well as his body.
> A certain amount of attention—but be careful to give your attention to the right things, not to the wrong.
> A feeling of power. Give them the satisfaction of achieving things for themselves and overcoming difficulties without too much assistance from you.[6]

So now, instead of being punished if he or she got their clothes dirty, children were allowed to get as messy as they liked while they skipped, bowled hoops, played games and enjoyed themselves. The days of elaborate, fussy clothes were over. Mothers were advised by magazine problem-page 'aunties':

> The frills and ruffles that used to decorate the dress-up frock are never seen on the smart child of today. I do not approve of fussy dressing, overdressing or dressing a child too old.'

Little girl wearing the more comfortable clothes of the early Twenties

What were the clothes thought to be suitable for a modern child? Very young children, parents were told, would be happiest in a 'romper' or 'creeper'—a one-piece romper-suit which fitted very loosely at the crutch for easy movement, worn with a floppy white sun-hat. Older boys wore very short trousers and loose shirts with either a jumper or a loose jacket which was long enough to almost cover their trouser bottoms. Little girls wore very short smock-dresses gathered high up on the chest from a shoulder-yoke, with short or long sleeves. All children wore brief

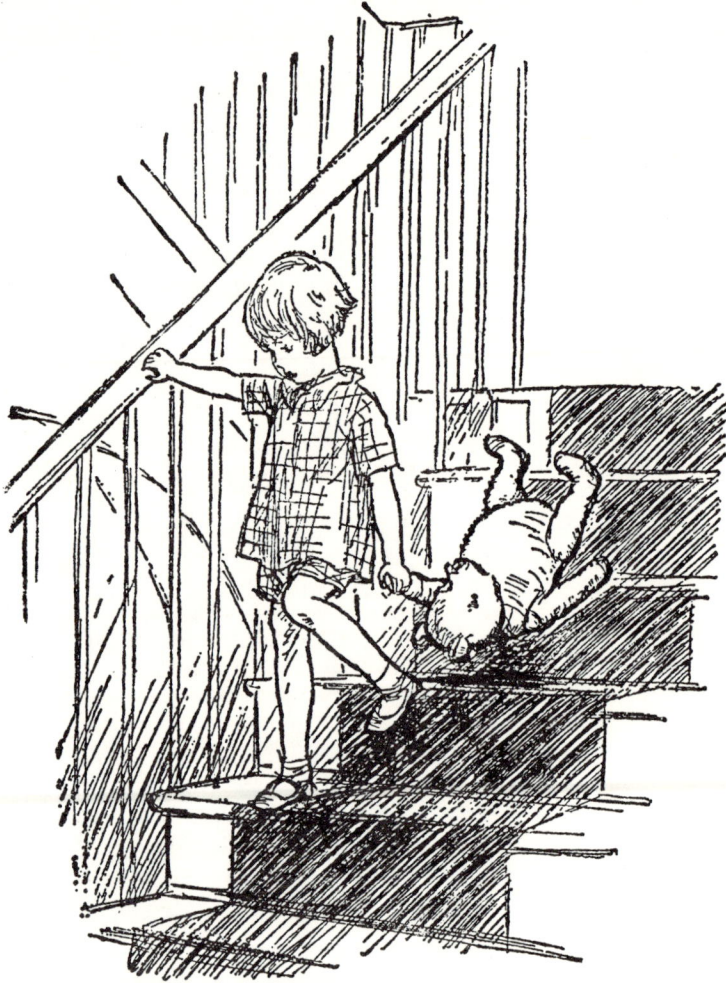

Christopher Robin with a Buster Brown haircut, loose smock and shorts, as illustrated in Winnie the Pooh

socks, ankle-length or mid-calf length, together with barred or lace-up shoes. In colder weather children wore expensive kid gaiters with their outdoor coats, if their parents could afford them. These went over their shoes like spats; they were buttoned up the outside of the leg using a button-hook. Later in the Twenties girls began to look more like their mothers in straight up-and-down dresses belted on the hips, with their hair bobbed short in the style of the cartoon character Buster Brown or shingled beneath

miniature cloche hats. Camiknickers were thought to be useful and hygienic under-clothes for girls. Both boys and girls now wore striped pyjamas for their bed-time pillow-fights.

Parties became an important and fashion-able part of children's playtime. Parents would put as much energy into organising their son's or daughter's fancy-dress tea as they did into their own 'Harlequin and Columbine' masked dances. A fashion writer of the time suggested the following hints:

For chilly little mortals, best frocks are often made of velvet in some pale shade, with puffed sleeves. Party dresses of crêpe de Chine, marocain, taffetas or georgette are trimmed with frills, tucks, pleats or rows of corded pipings, in the same material. Very little lace is used.[7]

Good costumes were essential, so Weldon's published a whole range of fancy-dress paper patterns especially for children.

In poorer, backward country areas you would still have seen children going about in heavy boots, darned black stockings and thick serge, while cheeky little East Enders would dress themselves up in their older brothers' and sisters' flashy finery. William Brown, the hero of the 'William' books, meets an East End girl called Eglantine and her brother Elbert while they are out in the country on a charitable church outing—the only way that

77545
Umbrella
8-16 yrs.

77539
Fairy Sunshine
8-14 yrs.

77511
The Mustard
Club
8-14 yrs.

75638
Buy British
Goods
10-16 yrs.

77550
The Desert Chief
10-16 yrs.

77518
Merrie
England
10-16 yrs.

77520
The New Health
10-16 yrs.

77515
Mexican or
Spanish
Dancer
10-16 yrs.

77543
Queen of the
Fairies
10-16 yrs.

77512
In Nelson's
Days
8-14 yrs.

77549
Parcel Post
8-14 yrs.

A few of Weldon's fancy dress patterns for children

William Brown walking with Eglantine and Elbert (William and Elbert have swapped caps)

poor city children ever had a holiday in those days:

> William liked the almost incredible frizziness of her over-crimped hair. He liked the dirty feather in her hat and the violet blue of her dress. He liked her white stockings and yellow boots. He found her altogether and entirely charming. Eglantine's brother Elbert was pale and undersized and wore a loud check cap that would have fitted a grown man.[8]

Children like Eglantine and Elbert couldn't help looking funny—they had to wear whatever they were given or could scrounge. But on the whole, the boys and girls of the Twenties had never had it so good.

1. James Laver: *Women's Dress in the Jazz Age*, 1964
2. *Punch*, 1920
3. (ref. Deborah Torrens: *Fashion Illustrated*, 1974)
4. (ref. Deborah Torrens: *Fashion Illustrated*, 1974)
5. Evelyn Waugh: *Brideshead Revisited*, 1945
6. *Home Magazine*, IPC
7. *Home Companion*, IPC
8. Richmal Crompton: *William Again*, 1923

The Party's Over: the Nineteen-Thirties

In 1926 there was a General Strike. All public services and transport came to a halt for ten days in sympathy with the coal miners who were campaigning for better wages and conditions of work. The dispute was eventually settled, but the Strike set the scene for more industrial unrest during the Thirties. Then, in 1929, the New York Stock Market went bankrupt. Many people lost all their money and the Wall Street Crash led to a slump in prosperity throughout the western world. Millions of people were laid off work when their companies went bankrupt, and the great Depression of the nineteen-thirties began. Many women gave up factory work and went back into the home, to make way for their unemployed menfolk. The Twenties party had come to an end and people were now suffering from the hangover; this is why the Thirties has sometimes been called 'The Aspirin Age'.

Even the rich had to tighten their belts, spending less and saving where they could, so their clothes became more practical. Women's skirts grew longer and waistlines returned to their natural position. The fashion world was affected directly by the Wall Street crash: ten thousand workers employed in the Paris fashion industry were made redundant. Even when the fashion trade recovered, it was never again quite as extravagant as it had been in the Twenties. Designers still created lavish gowns for the very rich and for Royalty, but they now thought in simpler terms which took into account more than ever the working life that many women were leading. They realised that people of different classes now had much more similar lifestyles than before: working in offices during the day; playing bridge, golf and tennis; camping, hiking, sailing small boats and caravanning at the weekend.

As people's everyday lives grew bleaker, they tried to escape more and more into a colourful fantasy world. They still went dancing a great deal. The Charleston was out of date now; instead you danced the 'Lindy Hop', the 'Big Apple' and the 'Shag'. And stage musicals became the rage. People went to the theatre to be captivated, not only by Noel Coward's songs and Gertrude Lawrence's performances, but also by the lyrics and melodies of Jerome Kern, Cole Porter and George Gershwin. But above all, they went to the cinema. Silent films were now a thing of the past; since 1929 there had been 'talkies' and you could now enjoy all the glitter and excitement of Hollywood musicals, extravaganzas like Busby Berkeley's *Golddiggers of 1935*, and later, the thrilling dancing of Fred Astaire and Ginger Rogers in films like *Top Hat*. The screen goddesses of the Thirties wore costumes designed especially for them by famous *couturiers*; Adrian was Hollywood's top designer and he helped to give many of the stars their individual appeal. Joan Crawford was instantly recognisable by her built-up shoulders, thick sooty eye-lashes and boldly-painted dark red mouth. Greta Garbo was known for her page-boy hair, trenchcoats and

The actress Joan Crawford wearing a dress built out at the shoulders with bows

Film star Marlene Dietrich in one of her favourite tailored suits

swan-like shoulders. Jean Harlow, the 'blonde bombshell' usually slid about in slinky, bias-cut, halter-necked satin gowns. Mae West showed off her Edwardian hour-glass figure in tight-fitting floor-length dresses which flared out from the knee. You always knew Marlene Dietrich by her swirl of cigarette smoke and manly, tailored clothes which somehow made her look even more female. Women all over the world did their best to copy these looks just as they had in the Twenties: they plucked their eyebrows thin, pencilled them, applied eye shadow, mascara, scarlet lipsticks and vaseline gloss, and adopted the hairstyles and mannerisms of their idols.

People tried to compensate for the greyness of the Depression by making their night-life something more formal and special. Women dressed up more in the evenings and everyone saved hard to buy a copy of one of the glamorous new-style evening dresses. Back in the Twenties a well-known *couturière* called Madame Vionnet had devised a new method of cutting out fabric pieces, which she called 'bias-cutting'. When one of her designs was

made up of bias-cut pieces, it had two advantages over ordinary cutting: firstly, the fabric shaped itself beautifully to the wearer's body, clinging wherever it touched; and secondly, the dress would stretch sufficiently for its wearer to be able to put it on over her head or step into it without needing a side, front or back opening. Using this new cut, designers were able to produce exquisite gowns in silk chiffons, satins and crêpes which clung around the bosom, waist and hips, going down to a 'swallow-tail' point at the base of the back and flaring out from the thighs into an elegant sweep of long skirt. These new-style dresses exposed the back more than ever before and women, instead of wearing a corsage (a small posy of flowers) at the front of their bodices, now pinned their flowers at the back. They even wore long strings of beads back to front! A new neckline was created to emphasise the plunging back— the 'halter neck', where the straps holding up the dress front joined at the back of the neck. With these evening dresses women wore one or two entire fox furs, head, feet, tail and all, or else they threw a fox fur cape over their shoulders. It was considered graceful to trail a coloured chiffon handkerchief from the fingers to echo the lines of the dress, or to hold a fan made from a single ostrich feather.

Not only did women copy the film stars; they were also influenced, perhaps more than at any other time, by what Royalty was wearing. In the 1930s there were many splendid State occasions. In 1934 the Duke of Kent married Princess Marina of Greece, and ten-year-old Princess Elizabeth (now Queen Elizabeth II) was a bridesmaid. Princess Marina was a very stylish lady and women everywhere were soon copying her custom of wearing two strings of pearls, and wearing 'Marina hats'. In 1935 the nation celebrated the Silver Jubilee of King George V and a colour known as 'Jubilee blue' became popular. In 1937, following the death of King George V and the subsequent Abdication of King Edward VIII to marry the American divorcee Mrs Wallis Simpson (herself a very elegant woman), King George VI was crow-

Queen Elizabeth and the Princesses Elizabeth and Margaret wearing the kinds of clothes everyone wanted to copy

ned. That year, 'Royal purple' became the rage. Most of the Royal Family were dressed by the same *couturier*, an Englishman named Norman Hartnell, who also dressed such famous actresses as Gertrude Lawrence and Evelyn Laye. He made popular the Victorian crinoline or 'picture-style' dress that Jeanne Lanvin had dreamed up in the Twenties and which Royal ladies wore for many years afterwards on State occasions. In 1935 fashion magazines wrote enthusiastically about this new style:

> Romance, sweet romance awaits us this summer: a flutter of fans in Jubilee ballrooms . . . the whisper of taffeta morning, noon and night; and a flurry of parasols over ravishing bonnets at Ascot and Lord's . . . We shall wear picture frocks that look like paintings by Vandyke, Rubens, and Velasquez; transparent flaring coats in tulle, organza . . . splendid coats of taffeta or brocade with tight waist and full skirts . . .[1]

This Royal, romantic look became even more popular when worn by film stars such as Vivien Leigh in the film *Gone With the Wind*, Greta Garbo in *Camille* and Norma Shearer in *The Barretts of Wimpole Street*.

In Paris, an Italian woman called Elsa Schiaparelli became *the* designer of the Thirties. She was world-famous both for her chic, elegant evening wear and for her extraordinary ideas. Many people nowadays have called her the Mary Quant of the Thirties and one writer of her own time described her clothes as being 'as new as technology, the sort of things that go with chromium-plated furniture'. She began her career making black sweaters with a realistic-looking white bow actually knitted into them—an optical illusion which everyone thought very clever. Schiaparelli disliked the sloping shoulders and fluid lines of the Twenties; she replaced them with her very own square-shouldered look, which she described like this:

> Up with the shoulders!
> Bring the bust back into its own, pad the shoulders and stop the ugly slouch!
> Raise the waist to its forgotten original place!
> Lengthen the skirt![2]

Schiaparelli yachting outfit, 1939

Schiaparelli sportswear, 1939

Her new look created a small revolution in the fashion world. One magazine reported in the spring of 1933:

> Skirts are not an issue anymore. Neither are waistlines. Shoulders *are* an issue. An issue? They are an avalanche! "There's nothing to get excited about in shoulders," you object. "Haven't we been wearing balloons on our arms for a year?" We have, but wait till you see the 1933 version.
>
> It has little to do with balloons, and is not a bit reminiscent of "leg of mutton" either. What it *is* is Egyptian, and Schiaparelli is its prophet . . . Some of her shoulders are jutting just like epaulettes, giving an appearance like one of Napoleon's marshals. One coat, which she wore herself, has a huge epaulette of brown monkey fur that runs right around back, sides and front, in a sort of continuous performance. Sometimes her models make you think of sixteenth-century nobles. If you are dressed by Schiaparelli this spring this is how you may look, or else like the Egyptians Rameses and Seti, modernised with a twentieth-century clown's hat![3]

Some of Schiaparelli's ideas were amusing as well as original. There were sweaters with skeletons on them; bathing suits with wriggling fish decorating the stomach; suits for flying and golfing; the first evening dresses made with matching jackets; tweed raincoats for evening wear; suits fastened with padlocks instead of buckles; dresses made from a pink glass fabric called 'Rhodophane'; buttons made to look like chains, clips, stars, moons, acrobats, lollipops and golden sovereigns; beach jackets done up with zips; wigs in shades of red, white and silver; material printed to look like newspaper; hats in the shape of high-heeled shoes and lamb cutlets! She even produced a necklace that looked like a string of aspirins.

When the actress Mae West wanted some clothes made, she sent Schiaparelli a life-size plaster cast of herself in the pose of the famous statue the *Venus de Milo*. Schiaparelli decided to make a scent bottle in the shape of this plaster cast when she launched her own perfume, 'Shocking'. And 'shocking pink' was the name she gave to her favourite shade of blue-pink—people have called it that ever since. Schiaparelli gathered around her the famous artists and designers of the time, men like Jean Cocteau and Salvador Dali, to produce exciting prints for her fabrics. Salvador Dali made a huge shocking pink stuffed bear, dressed up in jewels and a satin coat, with drawers in its stomach to hold clothes, for her salon. Everything to do with Schiaparelli's designs was fun and games.

In the Thirties, people were reading more and more as the first Penguin paperbacks were published, municipal public libraries were developed and glossy fashion magazines came into their own. They became highly influential, reporting on Paris collections, suggesting outfits for everyday, evening and cruise wear, telling the public what the Hollywood stars were wearing and at whose parties and which film première they had been seen. *Vogue, Harper's Bazaar, Femina, Women's Wear Daily* and *L'Officiel* could

Original coat-dress design from Paris

Advertisement for Schiaparelli's 'Shocking' perfume

between them make or break the success of a *couturier* or a particular style. During the late Twenties and all through the Thirties fashion photographers such as Cecil Beaton (who photographed Royalty and high society), Baron Adolph de Meyer and Man Ray made clothes look even more alluring through their artistic camera-work. And the top fashion magazine artists, Drian in the Twenties, Carl Ericsson (known as 'Eric') and Christian Bérard in the Thirties cleverly captured the mood of the age in their fashion drawings.

The clothes women wore became more 'womanly' during the Thirties. In the early years day dresses were worn with slim bias-cut skirts, but as the years passed skirts started to flare out and, as shoulders became more

Original coat design from Paris

sound-amplifying microphones. For these outings and for everyday wear the jacket-and-skirt costume was still an essential part of every smart woman's wardrobe. And there were some new coat shapes to throw over the top: three-quarter-length swagger styles with military epaulette shoulders, sporty blazers, thigh-length jackets and military trench-coats for wetter days.

Fashion's new, more curvy shape required different kinds of foundation garments. Now that women needed some form of bosom support, the company of Kestos produced the first modern-style brassière, with ribbon shoulder straps that crossed over at the back and came around to button under the bust in front. Corsets were worn all the time, even by slim women, but were now lighter and prettier than they had ever been as manufacturers began to make them with fewer uncomfortable bones and more stretchy elastic panels. The latest trend in knickers was what were known as 'French knickers', with wide, comfortable legs, in silk or satin.

puffed, padded and caped, women's waists appeared to look even smaller. A new kind of silky tea-time frock was advertised as 'just right for dancing, supper, and tea dates'. Over her tea-frock a woman might wear the latest short bolero. So important was cinema-going that fashionable women even wore a special outfit on their evening outings to the splendid new Odeon buildings. In April 1936 *Weldon's Good Taste* wrote:

'. . . the robe de cinema is ankle length, opened in front from neck to hem to reveal a foundation of different colour'.

However, the cinema was not the only popular form of entertainment. Those who could afford to used to drive off at the end of the working day in their cars (the Ford 'Tin Lizzie' was most people's favourite car at that time) to the new 'roadhouses' built on the main roads out of London. Here there were restaurants, swimming pools, dance floors and gardens—and you could stay there having fun until the early hours, listening to the new American-style 'crooners' singing through

Fashionable après-ski knitwear, 1937

73

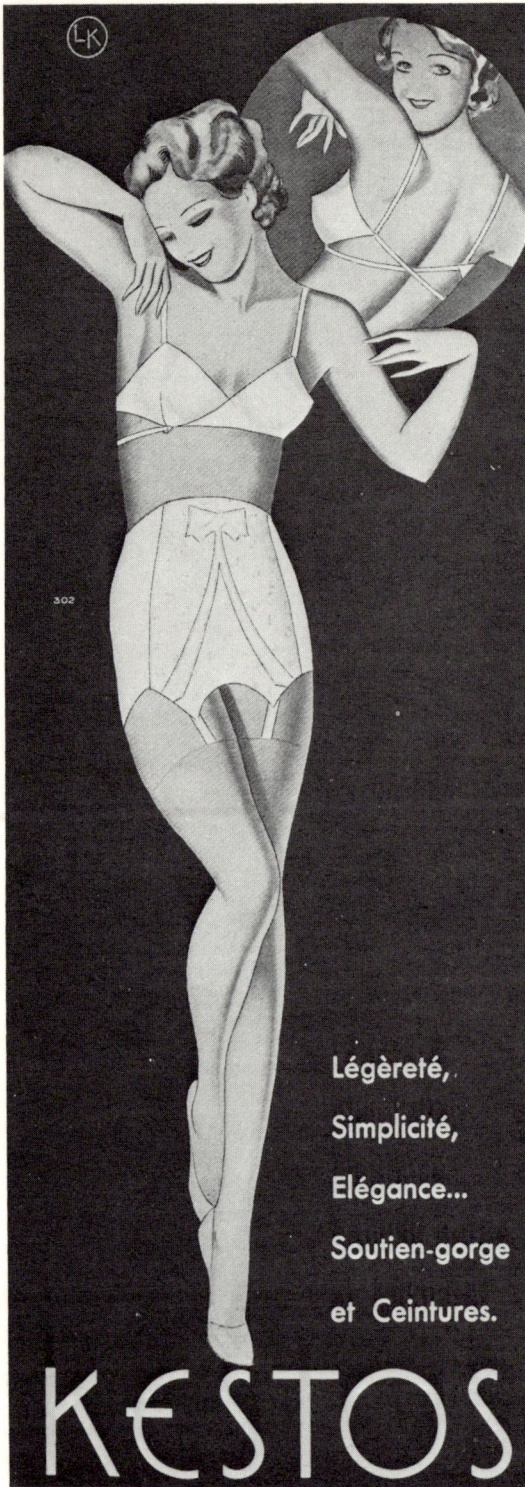

The original Kestos bra and girdle

The Chilprufe company was producing clingy vests and knickers which were warm yet thin enough not to spoil the outlines of women's dresses. Stockings were now worn in darker shades of rayon (these were the last years of rayon, for by the end of the Second World War women everywhere would be wearing nylon stockings, first invented in 1940).

Unlike the Twenties, the Thirties saw many changes in the colours considered fashionable. There were pastels everywhere in the early years of the decade, but later stronger, darker colours were worn: carmine red, Sherwood green, deep cyclamen and navy-blue. Many of the clothes imported from America were gaily patterned with floral prints, stripes, checks and polka dots. Like the clothes with which they were worn, shoes grew darker and heavier in shape, with more rounded 'barge' toes, and often with concealed elastic inside for greater comfort. There were now sling-backs and peep-toes, and in 1936 the Italian designer Ferragamo

The heavier look of the late Thirties—fur coat and clumpy shoes

introduced wedge heels. Elegant women wore gold or silver sandals in the evening, and in wet weather they either put rubber galoshes over their high heels or wore the new ankle-high, sheepskin-lined suède boots with crêpe rubber soles and zipped-up fronts. An expensive pair of ready-to-wear shoes would now cost you 12s 11d (0·64p) a pair, and you would probably buy to go with them a large, boxy handbag made on a frame with big handles and a clasped top.

Physical activity and sun-worshipping became a cult during the Thirties. We all take the World Cup and international sporting events for granted nowadays, but it was in the Thirties that different countries first became really competitive. The strong political dictatorships springing up all over Europe—led by Franco in Spain, Benito Mussolini in Italy and Adolf Hitler in Germany—placed great emphasis on physical fitness in young people, who were to be the citizens of the future.

KESTOS

Kestos swimsuits, halter-neck sunsuit and sundress

While Hitler's Youth League was drilling and parading in Germany and athletes all over the world were preparing to compete in the 1936 Berlin Olympic Games, in England a less competitive organisation, the Women's League of Health and Beauty (founded in 1930) was exercising its members on the principle that 'the trained body can supply the secret of a simple happy life'. Its members wore brief black satin shorts and sleeveless white satin blouses, designed by a West End designer. Even today, this outfit, which in those days was considered extremely go-ahead, would not look out of place in a gym.

All over England and the continent of Europe naturist clubs and health societies were set up to worship the human body, movement and the great outdoors. Richmal Crompton, in her book *Still William*, poked gentle fun at the intellectuals who were so enthusiastic about Greek Eurhythmics, and yet so unsuited to their energetic activities:

> Weedy males and aesthetic-looking females dressed in abbreviated tunics with sandals on their feet and fillets round their hair, mostly wearing horn spectacles, ran and sprang and leapt and gambolled and struck angular attitudes at the shrill command of the instructress and the somewhat unmusical efforts of the (very) amateur flute player.[4]

Youngsters and adults everywhere joined hiking and rambling clubs. Women took to their bicycles, carrying rucksacks, and wearing sports shirts made of a new open-weave cotton known as 'Aertex' with knee-length shorts (which grew shorter as the years passed) or divided skirts with a central inverted pleat. On the beach women were to be seen in two-piece costumes which were the forerunners of the bikini—but in the Thirties they only showed an inch or two of midriff and tummy. Women lounged about out of doors in sun-tops, sleeveless blouses, button-through play-suits and even backless sun-dresses—all the casual clothes we take for granted nowadays but which were rather daring in the late 1930s. People were beginning to walk around bare-headed in the sunshine and smart people were to be seen at the fashionable French resorts—Le Touquet, Cannes and Biarritz—wearing sun-glasses with round white or tortoiseshell frames to set off their sun-tans.

Men's clothes

Sadly, men's clothes grew duller and duller during the Thirties, with the exception of sports clothes, where coloured socks and shirts became fashionable. The Prince of Wales continued to set the trend. He favoured new American-style trousers (an early form of wide-legged hipsters). And he revived the fashion for wearing a white waistcoat under his dinner jacket. Patterned pullovers which had been worn for sports in the Twenties were replaced by plain ones or by Canadian-style 'wind-cheaters'—pouched over the waist and wrist-bands and zipped up the front. As with women's clothes, there was a feeling that it was healthier to wear fewer, more casual clothes, including shorts for athletics and hiking and 'Palm Beach' suits of light-coloured linen when the weather allowed, after the style worn by Humphrey Bogart in *Casablanca*. But men tended to be far more conservative than women, and business and social etiquette still dictated that they should wear heavy, dark suits, stiff collars, ties, and well-polished lace-up shoes when they went to the office; and, of course, a hat. (Sir Anthony Eden set the 'trilby' trend, but a hat with a 'snap brim', which you could turn up at the back and down at the front, was also very popular.)

A few younger, more eccentric men joined the 'hatless brigade' and walked about town in open-necked shirts and sandals, but this wasn't really 'the done thing'. Bohemians—writers such as D. H. Lawrence, artists such as Augustus John and members of smart literary sets such as the Bloomsbury group—were expected to look different from everybody else. You could usually tell an artist by his casual shirt, soft neckerchief, and even perhaps by a beard or by his French-style beret. In the same way, a writer would tend to wear ancient pullovers and crumpled tweed jackets which announced to the world that he

LORD BADINGTON
PRÉSENTE
sa magnifique collection de pardessus et
vêtements ready made, ville, voyage et
sport importés d'Angleterre.

LONDON HOUSE
62, AVENUE DES CHAMPS-ÉLYSÉES

The conservative look of men's clothes during the Thirties

Jaunty young man wearing a pullover tucked into his pleated-waist trousers

had thoughts far loftier than of going to the office! However, one or two men, such as the photographer Cecil Beaton, succeeded in combining a casual 'artistic' look with easy elegance.

Children's clothes

Children had become much more important. People were having smaller families, and as there were fewer servants, there was more interest in smaller houses, such as the new 'semi-s' in which large families were impossible. Parents pampered one or two children. They gave them constructive games like Meccano, potato printing equipment and paints to play with, and new comics and books such as *Rupert Bear* and *Winnie-the-Pooh* to read. Parents did everything they could to keep their boys and girls cheerful and happy. In fact, some of them thought that the new Walt Disney cartoons like *Snow White and the Seven Dwarfs* might frighten rather than please their children.

Like their parents, children were heavily influenced by Royalty and Hollywood. The Princesses Elizabeth and Margaret (together with their pet Corgi dog, Dookie) were followed, photographed and copied wherever they went and whatever they did. Most people felt that their family life was full of the 'simple homeliness' that everyone wanted in their own families. In 1932 a 'Margaret Rose' knitted frock, trimmed with rosebuds on the collar, sleeves and pocket, was shown in a magazine, in honour of Princess Margaret, and in no time at all every dutiful mother was knitting the dress for her daughter. The newspapers announced that Princess Elizabeth liked wearing primrose yellow and pink, so little girls after that were to be seen at the best tea-parties wearing fairy-like dresses in these colours, made of organdie, taffeta or net trimmed with frills and ruchings, and belted with a wide sash, then topped by a tiny cape thrown over the shoulders, like frocks worn by the Princess. The child idol in Hollywood was Shirley Temple, who won the hearts of millions with her sweetness and cute looks in films such as *Heidi*. Most mothers wanted their little girls to look like Shirley Temple or, if they were dark, like Judy Garland after she had appeared in *The Wizard of Oz*. Little boys, whether their parents liked it or not, swaggered around trying to be like the 'tough' boy star Mickey Rooney.

78

The young Princess Elizabeth with fashionable curls and a tiered organdie frock

Every mother's dream: Shirley Temple playing Heidi

While the children were small they all appeared much the same, lying in their wickerwork Moses baskets or in their smart, low-slung perambulators, wearing easily-washable frilly dresses, with their hair brushed into haloes of angelic curls. (As the magazines said, curly hair 'seems the natural frame for the curves of the chubby face, and it is worth any amount of care to keep it wavy'. If your baby didn't happen to have curls, there was an amazing new product called 'Curly Top' which would have his, or her, locks curling in next-to-no-time!) But as soon as they were beginning to stagger around on two feet, little boys had their curls cut off and were dressed in miniature 'manly' suits and ties, while little girls were expected to keep themselves neat and pretty in frilly dresses, looking just like William Brown's neighbour, Violet Elizabeth Bott:

"NOW YOU MUTH PLAY WITH ME," LISPED VIOLET ELIZABETH, SWEETLY.
"I DON'T PLAY LITTLE GIRL'S GAMES," ANSWERED THE DISGUSTED WILLIAM.

Violet Elizabeth's fair hair was not naturally curly but as the result of great daily labour on the part of the much maligned nurse it stood up in a halo of curls round her small head. The curls looked almost, if not quite, natural. Violet Elizabeth's small pink and white face shone with cleanliness. Violet Elizabeth was so treasured and guarded and surrounded with every care that her small pink and white face had never been known to do anything else except shine with cleanliness. But the *pièce de resistance* about Violet Elizabeth's appearance was her skirts. Violet Elizabeth was dressed in a white lace trimmed dress with a blue waistband, and beneath the miniature blue waistband her skirts stood out like a tiny ballet dancer's in a filmy froth of lace trimmed petticoats. From this cascade emerged Violet Elizabeth's bare legs, to disappear ultimately into white silk socks and white buckskin shoes.[5]

Violet Elizabeth's clothes sound very elaborate, and they were probably more complicated than most little girls' everyday dresses, for her newly-rich parents wanted her to look like a child star and to show off how wealthy they were. However, even very frilly dresses were not too difficult to look after in the Thirties, for children's clothes were now usually washable and designed to be pulled on and off quite easily.

But the rather jolly life enjoyed by many boys and girls soon came to an end with the outbreak of war in September 1939. Children living in large towns were evacuated, school by school, to the safety of the country and away from the dangers of bombing raids. Their parents had more important things to think about than amusing themselves and their children, for they were now threatened by the grim realities of the Second World War.

1. (ref. Deborah Torrens: *Fashion Illustrated*, 1974)
2. Elsa Schiaparelli: *Shocking Life*, 1954
3. (ref. Deborah Torrens: *Fashion Illustrated*, 1974)
4. Richmal Crompton: *Still William*, 1925
5. Richmal Crompton: *Still William*, 1925

A Mile of Shop Windows: How Clothes were Sold

What does buying clothes suggest to you? Probably you think of Saturday morning shopping in town for your everyday clothes; possibly an annual visit to the school outfitter, if your school has a formal uniform; perhaps, if you live in a remote country area, your parents look through a mail order catalogue and send away for new clothes by post. However you do your shopping, it is all very different from the ways of your great-grandparents. In their day there was no standard sizing—you could not just go into a

Early Butterick skirt patterns

shop and ask for a size 12, 14, 16 or small, medium, large, because no one would have known what these sizes meant. In the nineteen-hundreds every dress, blouse or pair of trousers had to be individually fitted to the customer. Stores sold their goods to the private dressmaker, lending out lengths of fabric 'on approval' for them to show to their clients; but stores also had their own workrooms where they kept details of the measurements and tastes of their individual customers together with patterns, fashion sketches of their own styles and copies of Paris original designs. They would make up to order and either deliver or send the garments by post to any part of the country.

Usually, when a woman ordered a made-up dress advertised in a store catalogue, she would be sent, not a complete dress, but a made-up skirt and a length of material for the bodice. For example, Swan & Edgar of Piccadilly advertised in 1907 a 'Smart Silk Robe (unmade), easily adapted to any figure' which could be 'easily fitted'—but we do not know whether the elaborate style was as simple to put together as the advertisement suggested. Peter Robinson advertised dresses completely made up apart from the back

Workers sewing tucks into skirts

Woman making pom-pom decorations in dark, bad conditions

seam, which was left open so that you could fit it to your own individual requirements. Sometimes the customer was asked to enclose with her order a well-fitting bodice of her own which the store workrooms would then use as a pattern.

To us, the clothes made in the nineteen-hundreds sound relatively cheap: D. H. Evans offered copies of a French model gown for twelve guineas, while at Dickins & Jones you could buy an exquisite tea-gown from five pounds upwards. Even for those days clothes were inexpensive, considering the amount of fine hand-work and intricate detail involved in making them. They were cheap because labour was cheap; most sewing work was still done by the patient fingers of overworked and underpaid seamstresses. Although the first sewing machines had been imported from the United States many years before, the best quality clothes were still sewn and finished by

hand, especially the exquisite Edwardian blouses worn then, with their innumerable tucks, lace insertions, pleats and frills. We know that the women who made these and other garments toiled from 8.45 in the morning until 7.30 at night, and all to earn miserable sums of money ranging between 4s 6d (0·22½p) to 22s (£1·10) a week, depending on their experience and position. The usual overtime rate was 6d (0·2½p) an hour. One old lady recalled working as a bodice hand in Swan & Edgar, where she worked for 12s 6d (0·62½p) a week (which rose to 15s (0·75p), then 17s 6d (0·87½p) later on):

Working hours were from 9 a.m. to 7.30 p.m. but to save money the girls [there were quite a lot of them in her area doing this kind of work] travelled up to Charing Cross on the last workman's train so as to get the 4d (0·1½p) cheap return fare. Arriving at 8, they filled in the gap by wandering round Covent Garden.

85

Ladies shopping outside the elegant entrance to Harrods of Knightsbridge

Lunch was sandwiches brought from home, but the firm provided tea and bread and butter. At 7.30 there was a stampede as they raced all the way from Piccadilly Circus to Charing Cross to catch the 7.40 train—encumbered by their long skirts and flannel and cotton petticoats, but smart in their buttoned boots with patent toecaps and, of course, hats perched on the padded-out hair drawn up to what was called a "teapot handle" on top. The ticket collector held the gates open for them and they often sang all the way home—they were all members of church choirs.[1]

Of course life was very different for the people who bought the seamstress's handiwork. Just before the turn of the century a writer noted that a very strong temptation was being set up for shoppers:

"the gathering together under one roof of all kinds of goods—clothing, millinery, furniture, in fact all the necessities of life . . . nearly all the great shops of London are becoming vast stores,

one of which, more entertaining than the others, is said to supply young men for dancing and coffins to bury them in". (That store was William Whiteley of Queensway.)[2]

People spent a great deal of time and took far more care shopping than they do nowadays, which is why they loved visiting the big new department stores being opened in big towns. All kinds of luxuries were provided for customers: heating, air conditioning, elegant chairs where you could rest after walking through the different departments; there was even an electric moving staircase in Harrods in 1898 for the convenience of customers. At the time of Harrods' Jubilee in 1909, the store boasted eighty departments. And, for the comfort of patrons there was a Gentleman's Club furnished in the Georgian style and a Ladies' Club in the Adam style, while afternoon tea was served to the musical strains of the Harrods Royal Red Orchestra!

86

Many wealthy people in the country and in the big manufacturing towns felt that shopping in their humble local shops was rather beneath them, but at the same time they were over-awed by the exclusive atmospheres of the top *couture* houses. They chose, instead, to travel into London to shop in one of these smart new stores. Here they could buy whatever they needed, carry out any banking business, dine in the restaurant, attend to their *toilette* in one of the luxurious cloakrooms and even visit an exhibition, all in the same building. In those days stores were open longer than they are now, from about 8.15 a.m. until 7.30 p.m. for six days a week.

Debenham & Freebody of Wigmore Street opened their newly rebuilt store in 1907 and so grand did it look, with its magnificent Italian marble columns, that they proudly referred to it as 'A Modern Drapery Palace'. Many of its products, including a selection of the finest lingerie, came straight from Paris. Debenham's boasted a special service: expert assistants would call on customers in the privacy of their own homes to assist them with their choice of purchases.

In 1909 Gordon Selfridge, an American businessman who had already successfully run a department store in Chicago, opened a vast new building in Oxford Street. He announced the fact by advertising on a scale never before seen in Britain, for he felt that his store was something new and special in London, with its banks of flowers, careful lighting, orchestras playing and windows which were lit up at night to show off the magnificent displays of colourful fashions. Above all, it was a store for everyone, even those of modest means: there was a bargain basement where, if you did not have much money, you could still afford a cheap pair of socks or a comb.

A much smaller establishment made its name selling specialised ready-to-wear fashion during the nineteen-hundreds. Thomas Burberry was the first draper to devote himself to producing sports and motoring clothes for

The original Burberry gabardine raincoat

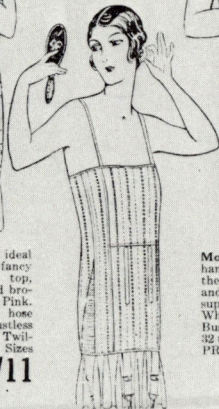

Twilfit corsets advertising the straight up-and-down look of the Twenties

women. As motoring meant travelling in dirt and mud, he designed roomy overalls or 'dust-wrappers', dust-proof motor veils and billowing curtains which served as a hat-cover, as well as all manner of motoring accessories. For playing golf he invented a 'free-stroke' coat with a special pivot sleeve so that the woman wearing it could easily lift and swing her golf club without ripping her armhole seams; it had a matching skirt which reached to the ground, but you could adjust the length using an ingenious system of loops and strings! The name 'Burberry' is associated, most of all, with a new cloth Thomas Burberry invented and patented, a weather-proof material which he called 'gabardine' and which is still used all over the world for making raincoats.

In the early years of this century stores and shops had many intriguing ways of dealing with money payments. Many stores installed a system called 'Lamson Pneumatic Tubing', whereby money and bills were sucked away from the counter and up to a central point in the store where change was given and sent back again to the customer. Other shops followed a rather quaint custom: the assistant, instead of giving the customer her farthing change, gave her instead a card of pins; and sometimes, in the less smart shops, a cheap farthing novelette was substituted for the farthing change. A farthing was worth less than a quarter of our present day $\frac{1}{2}$p.

During the Twenties, the ready-to-wear industry boomed, in spite of some unkind suggestions that ready-made dresses were as inferior as 'reach-me-down' clothes! If an exciting new style appeared in Paris, working women expected to be able to buy copies of it 'off the peg' in their high street store several months later, without having to bother about tiresome fittings. The big stores recognised this demand early on and spent large amounts of money advertising their ready-to-wear facilities. If you look through any of the old store catalogues, you will see over and over again phrases like 'the rush of modern life'. As communications improved—cars, aeroplanes, and the telephone system became bigger and better—life grew more hectic,

Motor delivery to-day—covering the country from Land's End to John o' Groats

One of John Barker's smart motor delivery vans

fashions came and went faster, and fashion-conscious shoppers increased in numbers. New suburbs sprang up around London and the big cities, so now special 'shoppers' trains' carried customers to and from town. The stores expanded their mail order services for those people who lived too far away to do their shopping in person. Barker's of Kensington proudly advertised the fact that 'a fleet of two or three-hundred motor vans now travel over half the country to deliver a parcel'.

The quality of clothes sold at this time varied enormously. Big stores were usually efficient and reliable; the small highly skilled workshops which produced their ready-to-wear goods kept up high standards, but the small shops which rushed in to make a quick penny produced badly botched garments which could only be relied on to stay in one piece for a short while. (Many years later, a similar thing happened: many of the little boutiques which sprang up in the 1960s to meet the needs of well-heeled trendy young people got away with selling roughly made, tatty clothes.)

When artificial silk or rayon was introduced in Britain by Courtaulds, under the trade name 'Celanese', the ready-to-wear trade expanded even further. Until then, the only clothes you could wash were those made of cotton and certain types of silk. But now new rayon 'washing frocks' were on sale in all the ready-to-wear shops and stores. In 1938 Joy's of Colchester advertised 'Activity frocks. Wash frocks made in crease-resisting rayon which looks like linen. All pastel shades and

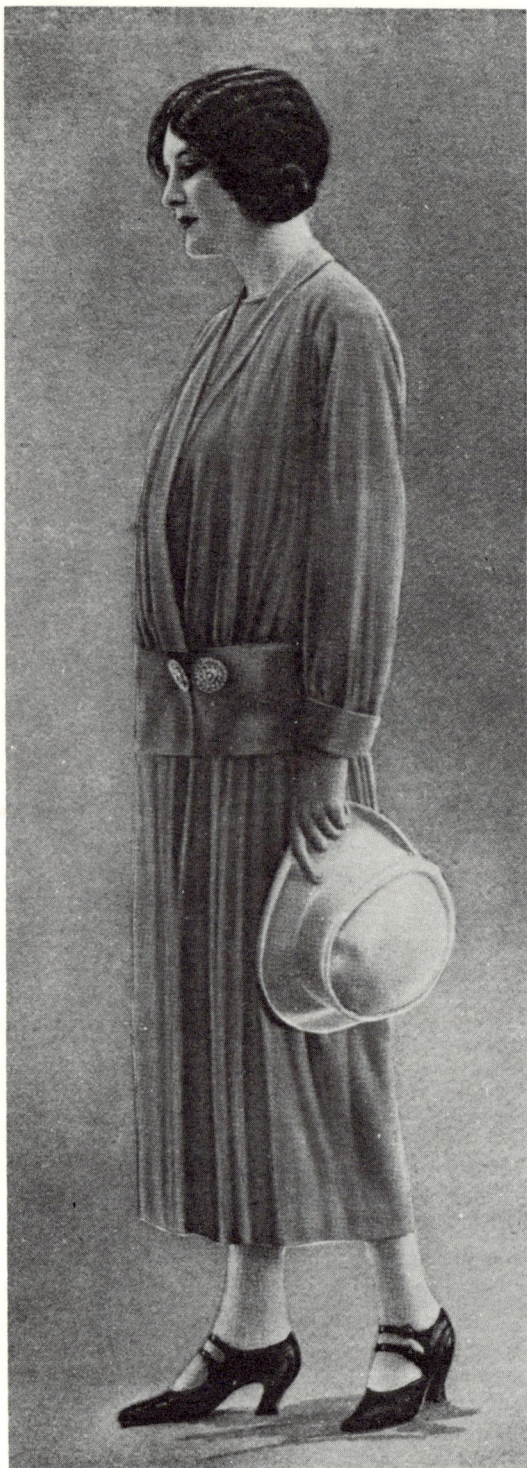

An early rayon dress

St Margaret—the ancestor of Marks & Spencer

navy, 9/11d.' Rayon stockings could be mass-produced far more cheaply than silk ones. One advertisement announced in 1921, 'Ladies' Artificial Silk Stockings. In black, white, nigger, grey and toney [flesh-pink]. Sold elsewhere 4s 6d. Our amazing price, 3s 11d.' (These early rayon stockings fitted the leg very badly and were coarse and shiny to look at.) Between the First and Second World Wars all kinds of new fabrics were invented, many of which have since disappeared. They had intriguing names like 'crêpe marocain', 'sharkskin', 'crêpoline', 'kasha', 'repp', 'sheenore', 'Wemble-chine', 'piqué', 'saxony', 'foulard' and 'georgette'). 'Tootal' and 'Tobral-co' were two of the new anti-crease, anti-

Courtaulds' Fabrics

Dress and Lingerie

are Fashion's Favourites.

It is sometimes hard to decide at once what kind of design or texture is most appropriate for a new frock or lingerie. You have only to go to your Draper or Store and ask to be shown some of the newest of COURTAULDS' FABRICS, and you will find every type in the widest possible variety. With COURTAULDS' FABRICS the making is straightforward, and the finished garment will give you lasting delight. Colours and textures are the best at every price and each Fabric carrying the well-known guarantee of the Manufacturers. The name is on the selvedge.

"Delysia"
Daintiness itself for present-day Underwear and Frocks.
37/38" wide, **3/11½d.** Per yard.

"Luvisca"
Looks like silk, is more durable than silk, and much cheaper than silk. 37/38" wide.
Striped designs **3/3d.** Per yard.   Plain or Self Checks **3/6d.** Per yard.

"Courcain"
A Rayon and Wool Marocain. Thoroughly dependable and hard-wearing.
38/39" wide. **4/11½d.** Per yard.

"Xantha"
The standard knitted fabric for Lingerie; beautifully soft and durable.
48/49" wide, **5/11d.** Per yard.

Illustrated are two dainty suggestions for "Luvisca."

San-Toy Printed Fabrics
Lovely colours and fascinating designs for the lady of taste, yet moderate in price.

"Courgette"
A delightful crêpe suède fabric, satisfying to the eye and pleasing to the touch.
36/37" wide, **6/11d. 5/11** Per yd.

"Clytie" SATIN
A luxury fabric at a moderate price, wonderfully durable in wear.
37/38" wide, **4/11d.** Per yard.

"Courlyn"
A high-grade Rayon and Wool Marocain of character and charm.
37/38" wide. **5/11d.** Per yard.

All the fabrics named are produced from Courtauld's finest Rayon yarns.

ASK TO SEE
"Viscolaine"
A NEW POPULAR-PRICED LINGERIE FABRIC.

Courtaulds' Fabrics
Dress and Lingerie

are obtainable from leading Drapers and Stores everywhere. If any difficulty, please write Courtaulds Ltd. (Dept. F.36), 16, St. Martin's-le-Grand, London, E.C.1. for name of nearest retailer and descriptive literature.

LINDSAY CABLE

The wide range of fine fabrics available from Courtaulds

'Celanese' of course !

WITH a glow of satisfaction you know your frock in 'Celanese' to be a triumph. It is lovely to look upon . . . its colouring is unusual and most attractive . . . it hangs with the natural grace of a 'Celanese' Fabric which at once gives a note of distinction.

For Evening Gowns, Day Frocks and morning wear, you can ring the changes right through the 'Celanese' Range. A wonderful choice of Fabrics . . . always practical . . . always inexpensively priced. Each frock will prove to be that paradox: "The nicest thing you have ever worn."

'CELANESE' DRESS SATIN
Width 38°
'CELANESE' CREPE-DE-CHINE
Width 38°/40°
'CELANESE' GEORGETTE
Width 38°/40°
'CELANESE' CREPE MONIX
Width 40°
'CELANESE' MAROCAIN
Width 40°

Ask to see the range of attractive 'Celanese' Printed Fabrics.

TRADE MARK

'Celanese' Fashion Fabrics

If any difficulty in obtaining supplies, write for name of nearest retailer to:
Sole Manufacturers: BRITISH CELANESE LTD., CELANESE HOUSE, HANOVER SQ., W.1
(Suppliers to the Trade only)

Celanese—the smart new synthetic

fade cottons which proved perfect for children's clothes.

All through the Thirties the United States led the world in clothes mass-production. Clothing experts brought over to Europe the American system of standardised sizing, so at last women could choose a garment which they knew would be likely to fit them, instead of buying on a basis of trial and error, as they had before. Outsizes were introduced for the larger man and woman. Vast quantities of American clothes were imported into Europe. Manufacturers started to produce ranges of clothes within a deliberately low price bracket; between 1932 and 1935 Guinea Gown shops were set up all over the country and carried on a flourishing trade. Here you could buy a dress for exactly a guinea (twenty-one shillings) and many of the dresses cost less than that. Middle-class women tended to look down their noses at these shops, preferring to buy their clothes in what they felt were the more respectable department stores; but for working women Guinea Gown shops were a boon. Where else could you buy 'dressy', yet inexpensive outfits for dancing and cinema-going?

The men's equivalent of the Guinea Gown shops were the Fifty Shilling tailors. During the Depression, even the most lowly office worker wanted to 'keep his end up' and look smart, to distinguish himself from the scruffy dole queues of the unemployed. He tried to dress like, and therefore look like, a gentleman. This helps to explain why men's clothes became so dull during the Thirties. The Fifty Shilling tailors (which later became the John Collier group), along with chains of shops like Montagu Burton and Hepworth's, all specialised in making and selling direct to the customer cheap versions of the basic Englishman's suit—dark grey, shapeless, respectable and dull. Other, more stylish companies such as Aquascutum and Jaeger developed along the same lines, making and selling suits direct to the customer through their own shops.

The dressy Thirties styles mass-produced for the Guinea Gown shops and stores seem far too fussy for most of our tastes nowadays. But we have to remember that in those days, when it was essential for a fashionable woman's outfit to be 'exclusive' or different from every other woman's dress, designers could only make their mass-produced garments look different by varying the trimmings (frills, pockets, cuffs and so on) on each one. Apart from the trimmings, the basic cut of clothes was much simpler during the Twenties and Thirties than it had been in the days of complicated, tightly-fitted Edwardian gowns. And it was because the cut of clothes became simpler that factories were able to develop new techniques of mass-production. Power-driven knives were now used to cut out

92

A battery of ten escalators conveys customers smoothly and quickly up and down to all six floors.

D.H. Evans' futuristic store design, 1937

Flowers, Spots and Checks give gaiety to these Washing Frocks

4 Attractive Styles all at 5'11

All these Frocks sent Post Free in Great Britain

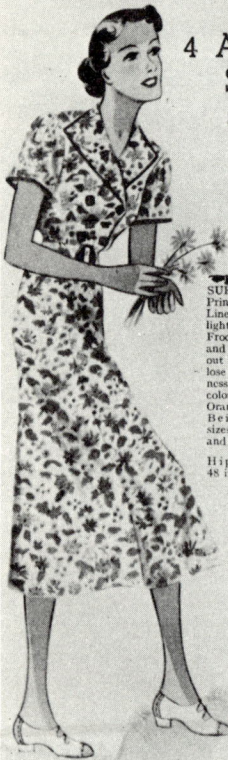

SUE Printed Imitation Linen makes a delightful little summer Frock that will wear and wash times without number and not lose its original freshness. In predominating colours of Blue, Green/Orange, or Green/Rose Beige. Hip sizes 38, 40, 42, and 44 ins. 5'11
Hip sizes 46 and 48 ins. 7'11

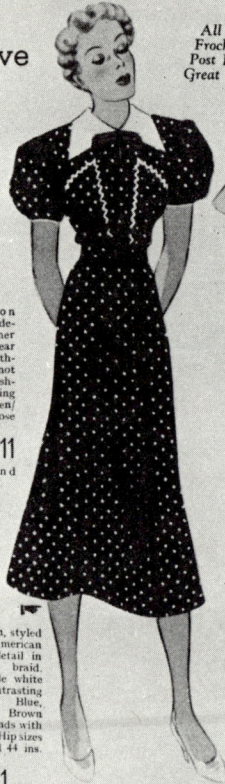

JANE Spotted Cotton, styled with an American crispness of detail in the tick-rack braid. Severely simple white collar and contrasting bow to tone. Blue, Navy, Green, Brown or Black grounds with a White spot. Hip sizes 38, 40, 42 and 44 ins. 5'11

PAT Printed Cottons are always right, always fresh and always useful. This one is in a gay floral design cut with a rounded yoke in contrast to the White, has pointed revers and sleeves just hinting at a puff. In predominating colours of Green, Brown, Blue or Black. Hip sizes 38, 40 and 42 ins. 5'11

MYRNA In Gingham, that needs no recommendation of its hard-wearing, 'easy-to-wash' qualities, this well-cut Frock buttons down the front and shows a distinct personality in the tailored revers and two 'dunce's cap' pockets. In check of White with Green, Brown, Blue, Cherry, Navy or Black. Hip sizes 38, 40, 42, and 44 ins. 5'11

Utility Frocks: 3rd Floor

D. H. EVANS—LONDON'S MOST MODERN SHOP   'Phone: MAYfair 8800   D. H. EVANS & CO. LTD., OXFORD STREET, LONDON, W. 1

Off-the-peg frocks that you could really wash and wear

pattern pieces. The Singer industrial sewing machine made sewing faster. Sophisticated machines were invented to lock-stitch, chain-stitch and finish hems off neatly. New steam presses put the final touches to the finished garments. Then they would be labelled with the company's brand-name and, sold wholesale to shops and stores, where they would be grouped on hanging rails according to size and style and sold over the counter to the customer. Using these modern methods, companies could translate original ideas into popular fashions in no time at all. My mother remembers rushing out to buy a 'Ginger Rogers' coat (it had a collar and buttons made from the dark curly fleece of a sheep called a 'caracul') after seeing the film star wearing it in her latest picture.

Many brands of clothing which are now household names started life in the Twenties and Thirties. 'Deréta'; 'Eastex'; 'Windsmoor'; 'Berkertex'; 'Alexon'; 'Rhona Roy'; 'Laura Lee'; 'Wendy Dresses'—all these originated during the ready-to-wear boom. Sometimes the companies concerned had their own designers, seamstresses and cutters working on the premises, but sometimes they would design an original model, then sub-contract the job of mass-producing the style out to teams of 'outworkers', small factories and workrooms of skilled cutters, machinists and finishers. Marks and Spencer worked in this way. The company (which began as a penny bazaar in the eighteen-eighties) began to concentrate, during the Thirties, on selling women's fashions in its multiple stores, using outworkers to produce the clothes, and has continued to do so ever since.

More and more skilled seamstresses, dressmakers and tailors became available in the manufacturing industries; many of the thousands of European refugees driven from their homelands by Adolf Hitler's oppressive régime came to settle in Britain. They made a great contribution to the British clothing trade, for they tended to have a sense of style and Continental expertise which many British designers and seamstresses lacked.

By the time war broke out in 1939, a whole new industry was catering to the needs and fancies of people who wanted moderately priced, stylish fashions for the ever-changing lives they were now leading. During the Second World War years everything, including clothes, was to be severely rationed, but in 1939 ordinary people could expect to find in the shops a more breathtaking choice of patterns, fabrics and styles than their parents would ever have imagined in 1900.

1. Elizabeth Ewing: *History of 20th Century Fashion*, 1974
2. Lady Jeune: 'The Ethics of Shopping', *Fortnightly Review*, January 1896

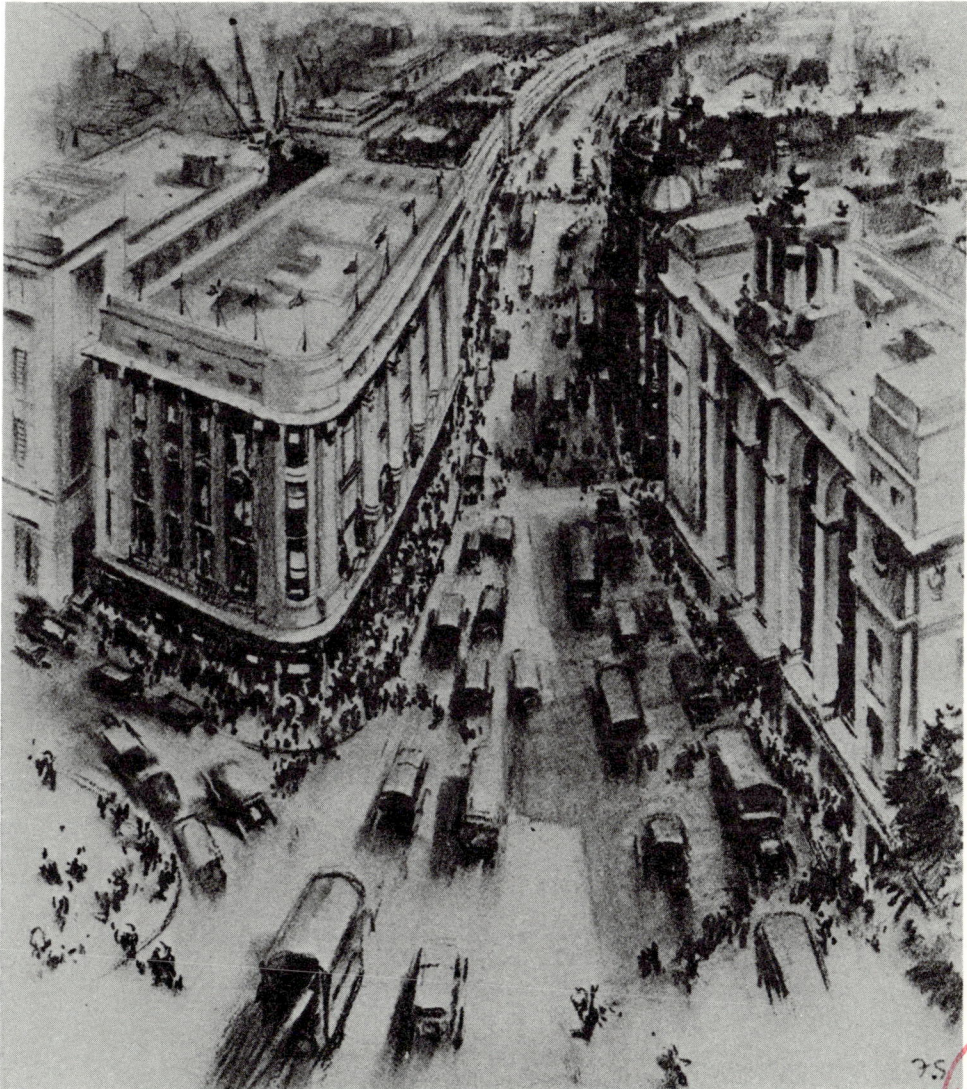

London's 'mile of shop windows': Kensington High Street in the Thirties

Acknowledgements

The publishers wish to thank the following for supplying the illustrations used in this book:

Bassano Vandyk, p. 31.
Ernest Benn Limited, p. 26.
Lafayette, p. 27 (top).
The Girl Guides Association, p. 48.
The Gluck family, pp. 30, 59.
The Hamlyn Publishing Group Limited, pp. 66, 81.
IPC, p. 65.
The Lampen family, p. 50 (top left and bottom).
The Collection of the Leeds City Art Gallery, p. 62.
The Raymond Mander and Joe Mitchenson Theatre Collection, p. 44.
The Mansell Collection, frontispiece, p. 17.
Metro-Goldwyn-Meyer Limited, p. 68.
The Museum of Costume, Bath, pp. 12, 15 (both), 27 (bottom), 32, 36, 38, 40, 42 and 43, 47 (both), 51, 52, 58, 60, 83, 86, 89, 90 (left), 93, 94, 95.
National Film Archive, pp. 69, 80.
Charlotte Newton, pp. 72 (right), 73 (left).
Popperfoto, pp. 84, 85.
Punch, pp. 16, 56, 61.
The Estate of E. H. Shepard, pp. 45, 64.
The Radio Times Hulton Picture Library, pp. 29, 46, 57.
Mrs Eva Reichmann, p. 20.
Twentieth Century Fox, p. 80.
The Victoria and Albert Museum, pp. 18, 21, 22, 24, 33, 35 (both), 37.
The Whiteman family, pp. 63, 78.
Wycombe Abbey School, Bucks, p. 49.

The publishers have been unable to trace the copyright holder of the illustrations on pp. 10, 11, 13, 23, 39, 50 (top right), 55, 70, 71 (both), 73 (bottom), 74 (both), 75, 77, 79, 87, 88, 90 (right), 91, 92. The originals are all in the possession of the author.

Photography by Chris Ridley

The cover photograph shows fashionable knitwear adorned with Cubist designs and is reproduced by courtesy of the Radio Times Hulton Picture Library.